Poems for the People

Carl Sandburg

Poems for the People

Edited with an Introduction by
GEORGE AND WILLENE HENDRICK

Chicago
Ivan R. Dee
1999

Library of Congress Cataloging-in-Publication Data:
Sandburg, Carl, 1878–1967.
    Poems for the people / edited with an introduction by George and
Willene Hendrick.
        p.   cm.
    Includes bibliographical references and index.
    ISBN 1-56663-236-6 (alk. paper)
    I. Hendrick, George.   II. Hendrick, Willene, 1928–   .
III. Title.
PS3537.A618A6   1999
811'.52—dc21   98-44501

Contents

Introduction   3

Don MacGregor   21
   Don MacGregor's Curse   30
   Memoir of a Proud Boy   31

Images and Colors   35
   Moon Dance   39
   Sunday   40
   Wings   41
   Li Po and Lao Tse Come to Nebraska   42
   Fire Flowers   43

Chicago   45
   [Two-Dollars-a-Day Wop]   52
   Crayon   53
   [Wilderness Man]   54
   Speed Bug   55
   Selling Spiel [on Maxwell Street]   56
   Good Woman   57
   Now You Take Her   58
   Bonbons   59
   The Lower Register   60
   Studio Saturday Afternoon   61
   A Long Shot   62
   Young Woman   63
   Sandburg to Loeb   65

Sense and Nonsense   67
    The Fleas of Flanders   71
    The Pie-Wagon Driver   73
    [Lullaby]   75

An Indian Legend   77
    [Pass This Baby On]   80

Character Studies and Personalities   81
    Terry Hut   84
    Daniel Boone   85
    Theodosia Burr   86
    Alice and Phoebe Cary   87
    Elbert Hubbard   88
    [Davvy Tipton]   89
    Socrates   90
    Stephen Crane   92
    Who Was Hannah Adams?   93
    [Tom Edison]   94
    John James Audubon   95
    Stephen Pearl Andrews   96
    Iron Jaw   97

Protest Poems   99
    Billy Sunday   104
    Both Ways   107
    [Finger Pointer]   108
    [Wreck a Bank]   109
    [Portrait of a Lady]   110
    A Talk with God   112
    Quotes   113
    On Account of This Is a Free Country   114

Nature Poems   117
    The Last Star   120
    Fires   121
    February   122

October   123
November Nocturne   124

Literary and Movie Criticism   125
[He Sez / I Sez]   129
Good and Bad Poets   130
[Henry James]   131
Successful Films   135

African-Americans   137
[A Goner]   141
[Love or Cheap Love]   142
John Arthur Johnson   143

World War I   145
May, 1915   149
[Lilacs of 1917]   150
Christmas Cartoon, 1917   151
Everybody in Town Has Been Drillin' and Drillin'
    for the Big Parade   152
The Woman on the Billboards   154

Ruminations   155
Acknowledgments   160
Climbers   162
Pigeons   163
Two Shapes in Gray   164
Two Girls and a Father   165
Palooka and Champ   166
Green Hair   167
Mulligatawney   169
Mutt Born   170
[Walt Whitman]   171

Toward The People, Yes   173
They Don't Know It Yet   176

Works Cited in the Introduction and Commentary   179
Index to the Introduction and Commentary   181

Poems for the People

Introduction

During the winter of 1914 a journalist-poet named Carl Sandburg and his wife, Paula, sister of the photographer Edward Steichen, decided to send a group of his poems to Harriet Monroe's Chicago magazine *Poetry: A Magazine of Verse*. The subeditors Alice Corbin Henderson and Eunice Tietjens were the first readers and were enthusiastic about these unconventional poems. They urged Monroe to accept them. At first Monroe hesitated, as Penelope Niven has noted in her biography of Sandburg, because of "their unorthodox form and their range from brutality to misty lyricism." But Monroe did see the poems as fresh and original and published nine of them in the March 1914 issue of her magazine.

The lead poem for that issue of *Poetry* was "Chicago," which began:

> Hog Butcher for the World,
> Tool Maker, Stacker of Wheat,
> Player with Railroads and the Nation's Freight
>   Handler;
> Stormy, husky, brawling,
> City of the Big Shoulders:

> They tell me you are wicked and I believe them, for I
>   have seen your painted women under the gas
>   lamps luring the farm boys. . . .

These and other lines of the poem came as a "shock" to Harriet Monroe, but she "took a long breath and swallowed it." Monroe's motto for *Poetry* was from Whitman: "To have great poets there must be great audiences too." She obviously felt that her discovery of Sandburg, who had never before been published in a major journal, was a promising new find and that Sandburg would have a large readership. Eunice Tietjens, however, wrote that the poems "roused a veritable storm of protest over what was then called their brutality. Many Chicagoans were furious at seeing their city presented in this, to them, unflattering light. . . ." It wasn't just Chicagoans who were offended by Sandburg's poetry. The *Dial* attacked the "hog butcher" school of poetry, finding "no trace of beauty in the ragged lines," whose style "admits no aesthetic claim of any description, and acknowledges subordination to no kind of law."

In the next issue of *Poetry*, Monroe defended the unorthodox poet Sandburg. As an editor she was willing to take chances, she said, to make "room for the young and new" and to "break the chains which enslave Chicago to New York, America to Europe, and the present to the past." Her gamble succeeded: Sandburg soon received the Helen Haire Levinson Prize for the best poems of the year, and he began to have an appreciative audience. While some of his poems dealt with social protest and the raw life of the city, others such as "Fog" were pure images which, once read, were not forgotten:

The fog comes
on little cat feet.

It sits looking
over harbor and city
on silent haunches
and then moves on.

Alice Corbin Henderson had recommended Sandburg's poetry to Alfred Harcourt, then a young editor at Henry Holt and Company. Harcourt was enthusiastic about most of the poetry but felt he would have difficulty getting the more radical poems approved by the conservative senior editors. Sandburg, then in his radical Socialist phase, had included in his manuscript several extremely revolutionary poems, including "Dynamiter":

> I sat with a dynamiter at supper in a German saloon
> eating steak and onions.
> And he laughed and told stories of his wife and
> children and the cause of labor and the working
> class. . . .
> His name was in many newspapers as an enemy of the
> nation and few keepers of churches or schools
> would open their doors to him. . . .

Harcourt questioned the radical tone of some of the poems, including this one. In a letter of February 4, 1916, to Harcourt, Sandburg defended the poem: "You placed a question mark on 'Dynamiter.' I would say put it in. I believe the backing for this book will come from the younger, aggressive fellows, in the main. Without tying it up to any special schools or doctrines, the intellectual background of it takes color from the modern working class movement rather than old fashioned Jefferson democracy." The poem was published.

Heeding Harcourt's advice, however, Sandburg did make changes in his scathing attack on pseudo-religion in a poem called "Billy Sunday." Harcourt believed that some of "the poems, the subjects of which are living people referred to by name, should certainly be omitted." Sandburg's slashing attack on the evangelist Billy Sunday, while not omitted, was somewhat tempered. The title became "To a

Contemporary Bunkshooter." Sunday was not named in the poem, and other deletions made it acceptable to the Holt publishing firm. In his letter defending the revised poem, Sandburg wrote to Harcourt on February 4, 1916: "The only other American figure that might compare with Sunday is Hearst. Both dabble in treacheries of the primitive, invoke terrors of the unknown, utilize sex as a stage prop, and work on elemental fears of the mob, with Hearst the same antithesis to Tom Jefferson that Billy Sunday is to Jesus of Nazareth."

Sandburg was finally allowed to include, sometimes in revised form, many of the social protest and anti-war poems that Harcourt had questioned. When Holt finally published *Chicago Poems* in 1916, reactions and reviews were mixed. The conservative critic William Stanley Braithwaite thought it was a "book of ill-regulated speech that has neither verse or prose rhythms." He did believe, however, that Sandburg had a "strong if unpleasant imagination, which is strangely woven with a tenderness that is striking." The *New York Times* reviewer judged the work to be "all alive, stirring, human. The best is very good indeed; the worst is dull and shapeless. But the worst can easily be let alone, for there is so much of the good."

Living up to Harriet Monroe's belief in him, Sandburg did indeed quickly find a wide audience among the masses for whom his poetry was deliberately written. How did he do this? How did he become a poet of the people and for the people?

Carl August Sandberg was born on a cornhusk mattress in a small cottage in Galesburg, Illinois, on January 6, 1878. He was the second child and first son of August and Clara Sandberg, both immigrants from Sweden. August took the name Sandberg after he came to Illinois, where he worked for many years as a blacksmith's helper at the Chicago, Burlington & Quincy Railroad shop in Galesburg, then a small town of about fifteen thousand with many immigrants. In Sweden his family name was Danielson, or perhaps Sturm, or was it Holmes? Carl was never able to learn the original family name. Later the children in the family adopted the spelling Sandburg, and Carl, as part of his Americanization, for many years used Charles instead of Carl for his first name.

The elder Sandberg worked ten hours a day for fourteen cents an hour. He was a quiet, undemonstrative man, fearful of poverty. He could read Swedish but could not write. He never attempted to perfect his English. His wife, Clara, had come to Illinois as a hotel maid. She learned English more easily than her husband. The elder Sandbergs spoke Swedish at home, and Carl learned Swedish before he could speak English. August had little interest in "book learning." Clara, though, supported her children's interest in education. Carl saw her as a kind, bighearted woman.

Sandburg wrote perceptively about his early years in *Always the Young Strangers*. There were seven Sandberg children (two boys died young), and funds were always short. Young Charlie delivered newspapers and did janitorial work to help the family income. He was a bright boy, a good student, curious about whys and wherefores. He was a reader and a dreamer.

The Sandbergs were Swedish Lutherans, and August was a staunch Republican in a strong Republican region. But young Charles had a friend, John Sjodin, who was "a hard-and-fast political-action radical. 'The big corporations' were running the country, as John saw it, and the time would come when the working people, farmers and laborers, would organize and get political power and take over the big corporations, beginning with the government owner-ship of railroads. Always John was sensitive about the extremes of the rich and the poor, the poor never knowing what tomorrow would bring and the rich having more than they knew what to do with." Although Sandburg did not become a Socialist at that time, Sjodin started him thinking about politics, business, and crime in America.

When young Carl finished the eighth grade in 1891, he quit school and went to work at a series of dead-end jobs, contributing money to the family treasury. He seemed no different from millions of young working-class adolescents in America then. Unsure of himself and his future, he tried one job after another: milk delivery boy, newspaper boy, shoeshine boy, and as a hobo in Iowa, Kansas, Nebraska, and Colorado he was a farmhand, dishwasher, odd-job man. Sandburg gives a vivid picture of those years in *Always the Young Strangers*; even as an adolescent with no goals in life, no long-term plans, he was a careful observer of the people he met and the events he saw.

In 1896, at the age of eighteen, Sandburg went to Chicago for the first time. His father got him a pass on the "Q," as the Chicago, Burlington & Quincy Railroad was known. Charlie had a dollar and fifty cents, but John Sjodin, who knew the city, told him how to live cheap, and cheap it was. He stayed three days. His flophouse charge was twenty-five cents a night; breakfast at Pittsburgh Joe's was wheat pancakes, molasses, margarine, and coffee, five cents. At the same diner his lunch and dinner were identical: a bowl of meat stew, bread, and coffee—ten cents a meal. For three days he walked: he saw the department stores and the newspaper offices where the papers he had carried in Galesburg were edited; he saw for the first time a large body of water; he observed the Board of Trade activities. Mostly, though, it was the "roar of the streets" that fascinated him, just as the movement of people and traffic in Manhattan had fascinated Walt Whitman.

On his last day in Chicago Charlie went into a saloon that featured a free lunch. He paid his five cents for a glass of beer, which he accompanied with rye bread, cheese, and baloney. While he was eating and drinking a woman came up and took a chair at his table. She appeared young, but there were "hard lines at the mouth and eyes."

As Sandburg reconstructed the scene many decades later, "She smiled a hard smile and said, 'What are yuh doin? Lookin fer a good time?'"

"I said, 'I'm polishing nail heads for Street and Walker.' It was a saying then. If you were out of work and looking for a job you walked the streets where the wooden sidewalks had nail heads sticking up and your shoes polished those nail heads.

"Her face lighted up and she blazed it at me, 'I'm goin to polish your nail head fer yuh!' She was terribly alive and the words came hard through her teeth and her pretty mouth.

"I waited a few seconds fumbling around with what to say and then told her, 'You're up the wrong alley, sister, I ain't got but two nickels and they wouldn't do you any good.' She stood up, said, 'All right' cheerily and skipped along toward men at other tables."

In three days the young Sandburg saw much of the city he was to write about in his 1914 poem "Chicago," including painted women luring country boys.

Sandburg might have remained a bright man working only dead-end jobs all his life except for one event—the Spanish-American War. When the hostilities began in 1898 he enlisted in Company C, Sixth Infantry Regiment, Illinois

Volunteers. Private Sandburg saw duty in Puerto Rico and then returned home to Galesburg. As a veteran he was offered, for the first year, free tuition at Lombard College in his hometown. Lombard had been founded by the Universalist church and was theologically and academically liberal. It had a small enrollment, usually under two hundred, a good faculty, and sponsored a great many extracurricular activities. Sandburg had never expected to go to college; as fate would have it, he was a student at just the right institution. Because he had not attended high school, he was enrolled as a special student and allowed to take makeup classes as well as regular college classes. He threw himself into college life.

To make money for books and other expenses, Charlie signed on as "call man" for the fire department. He slept at the fire station nights and left his classroom if a fire broke out during the day. He was paid ten dollars a month. He ate his meals at home and had a hall bedroom in the family house as a study. After his first year of college, he worked at odd jobs to pay his tuition for the next years. In his four years at Lombard, 1898–1902, Sandburg received a fine liberal arts education, as he reported in the second volume of his autobiography, *Ever the Winds of Chance*, unfinished at the time of his death in 1967 and finally published in 1983. He read and pondered major literary texts, took an intensive composition course ("Daily Themes"), studied Latin, chemistry, history, sociology, and religion. He gave orations, acted in plays, played on sports teams, most notably basketball, was business manager, then editor-in-chief of the literary magazine *The Lombard Review*, and was coeditor of *The Cannibal*, the college yearbook.

These were years of intellectual ferment and social maturity for Sandburg. The great influence upon him during this time was Professor Philip Green Wright, a brilliant teacher of composition, economics, astronomy, and mathematics, who invited students to his house to discuss literature. In Sandburg's last year at Lombard, Wright "organized 'The Poor Writers' Club,' saying we were poor, and we were writers, so why not?" Wright was a Socialist, "closer to . . . William Morris than to Marx." John Sjodin had introduced Sandburg to socialism, but Wright moved Sandburg more firmly into that camp. The Lombard professor was also a poet and encouraged Sandburg to become a writer. Sandburg correctly saw Wright as one of the major influences on his life, career, and philosophy.

Sandburg left college without taking a degree. In the four years since his army service he had changed greatly. He had improved his writing skills, had read widely, and had discovered the poetry of Whitman, which would influence his own poetry. Through participation in elocution courses and drama performances, he began to recognize his own abilities as an orator and actor. He took advantage of the cultural opportunities on the Lombard and Knox College campuses in Galesburg; he got cheap seats for lectures and plays in the Auditorium in downtown Galesburg. He was now an educated man, but instead of entering a profession he began some wandering years, a life of self-education among the people. While at Lombard one summer he had sold Underwood & Underwood stereoscopic photographs. After leaving college in 1902 he moved around the country selling these stereoscopic views, working just enough to meet his simple needs. In his spare time he read in public libraries or borrowed books and worked at his poetry and prose. He "rode the rails" and served time in jail for traveling without a ticket.

In 1904 he returned to Galesburg, wrote a column for the local newspaper, and put together his first book, *In Reckless Ecstasy*. Philip Wright had a hand printing press in his basement and published it as a pamphlet. Sandburg had not yet found his style and his voice in this early work, and it was not a success. He was still a wanderer and a seeming idler, but he was now seriously committed to becoming a poet.

In 1905 he went to Chicago again and got a job as an assistant editor of *Tomorrow Magazine,* where he published both his own prose and his own poetry. As a way of supporting himself, he turned to lyceum lecturing, working up programs on Walt Whitman and George Bernard Shaw. His socialism at the time was similar to that of Shaw and the Fabian movement in England.

Still uncertain about how he should support himself, in 1907 Sandburg became an organizer for the Social Democratic party in Wisconsin. Soon after taking that position he met the beautiful Socialist Lilian Steichen. Theirs was a passionate and intellectual courtship, largely by mail, and they were married in June 1908. (Margaret Sandburg, their oldest daughter, edited their love letters in *The Poet and the Dream Girl.*) Paula (as Sandburg called Lilian) was convinced that Sandburg was a poetic genius. She was an excellent critic of his writing and, like Wright, a major influence on his thinking and on his poetry, as was her brother, the artist and photographer Edward Steichen.

In the early years of their marriage, the Sandburgs moved about continually doing Socialist work. Sandburg wrote numerous articles and pamphlets for the cause and worked for Eugene Debs in his candidacy for president.

In Milwaukee he began to write for Socialist newspapers, and in 1910 the Socialist mayor appointed Sandburg his private secretary. With Paula's encouragement he continued to write poetry and began to develop his own distinctive voice.

Sandburg's reputation as a journalist was growing, and

in 1912 the Sandburgs left Wisconsin and moved to Chicago. There he first worked on the Socialist paper, the *Evening World*, and then *The Day Book*, an ad-less, left-leaning paper. The radical journalist Don MacGregor was city editor there, and the two became friends. Sandburg also fell in with more radical Socialists and began to publish, often under assumed names, in the *International Socialist Review*. Philip R. Yannella has traced this radical phase of the poet-journalist in *The Other Carl Sandburg*.

Several of the poems in the collection that follows belong to this period in Sandburg's life—his earliest years after he moved to Chicago in 1912. We know that he knew IWW leaders such as Big Bill Haywood and the dynamiter Anton Johannsen, but he also made influential literary friends: Vachel Lindsay, Theodore Dreiser, Edgar Lee Masters, Sinclair Lewis, and Amy Lowell. Lombard had been the right college for Sandburg's young years. Chicago, with its teeming life and literary ferment, was the right city for him in his early maturity. He flourished in the Windy City.

Working as a reporter in Chicago, he began to write poems as a kind of daily diary. He roamed the city and its byways. He spent many evenings at the bohemian Dill Pickle Club, founded by Jack Jones, reputed to have been a safecracker early in his life. That club on the Near North Side of Chicago had a sign at the door: "Step High, Stoop Low, Leave Your Dignity Outside." Inside was a cartoon of a man shouting, "We gotta change the system." The clientele of the Dill Pickle appealed to Sandburg: tycoons, pickpockets, artists, hoboes, thieves, professors, politicians, hopheads, whores, social workers, labor organizers, writers. Sandburg went to the theater, visited galleries and museums, and was a regular visitor at the offices of *Poetry*. He was a part of the artistic, social, and economic ferment of those years just before and after World War I, but he was also a private person, contemplative, musing on the world around him, writing nature poetry. It was in this exhilarating atmosphere that Sandburg came to poetic maturity.

After publishing *Chicago Poems* in 1916, Sandburg quickly completed three other volumes of poetry: *Cornhuskers* (1918), *Smoke and Steel* (1920), and *Slabs of the Sunburnt West* (1922). By 1936, when he published *The People, Yes*, his most active poetic period was over.

Sandburg opposed World War I in its early phases, writing notable anti-war poems. Socialists in the United States were divided over support of American involvement in the European war, but when the United States entered the war Sandburg joined those who supported President Woodrow Wilson. Yet he continued to write articles in the *International Socialist Review* (under the name Jack Phillips) upholding part of the Socialist agenda. He was "zigzagging in wartime," as Philip Yannella properly points out in *The Other Carl Sandburg*. He was torn between his strong anti-war sentiments and his equally strong need to support his country at war.

In the final months of World War I, after many difficulties caused by wartime red tape, Sandburg became a foreign correspondent for the Newspaper Enterprise Association and was stationed in Sweden. Many of the stories he sent back to his editors were sympathetic to "the Bolsheviks [the successful Russian revolutionaries] and the failed revolutionaries of Finland." One of Sandburg's major sources for information at the time was Mitchell Berg, born Gruzenberg, who finally assumed the name Mikhail Borodin. He was later Stalin's agent in trying to introduce China to communism. When the war ended in November 1918 and Sandburg was scheduled to return home, Berg asked him to take documents and films about the Bolsheviks back to the United States. Berg also asked Sandburg "to deliver $10,000 in bank drafts to Santeri Nuroteva, the head of the Finnish Socialist workers information office in New York" and to take a small sum to Berg's wife, still residing in Chicago. Sandburg for some reason then went to see officials in the United States legation to report on materials he was carrying with him, but he refused to indicate the source of the $10,000 in bank drafts. When Sandburg arrived in New York on Christmas Day, 1918, American officials, suspecting that Nuroteva was an agent of Lenin's, interrogated Sandburg and seized the bank drafts and many of the films and documents he had brought with him from Sweden.

Sandburg thought he had acted as a responsible journalist and was protecting his sources when he refused to say who had given him the $10,000. Although he was not prosecuted, he found himself in serious legal trouble.

Liberals and radicals who had supported the Russian Revolution were suspect in the years immediately after the war. As Attorney General A. Mitchell Palmer began to harrass liberals and radicals, raiding their homes and offices, Sandburg began to move away from his earlier radical views. Just why he did this cannot now be determined with any certainty, but he does seem to have been frightened by the political mood in the United States. Still, he remained a man with a strong social conscience throughout the rest of his long life. Politically he became a New Deal Democrat, and he supported Presidents Roosevelt, Truman, Kennedy, and Johnson.

In the early 1920s Sandburg turned to writing imaginative stories for children, stories that were for him a refuge from a world teetering on madness: *Rootabaga Stories* appeared in 1922, followed by *Rootabaga Pigeons* the next year. His biography of Lincoln, *Abraham Lincoln: The Prairie Years* in two volumes (1926), which he originally intended for children, was safely outside the political scares of the twenties. He had joined the *Chicago Daily News* staff not long after he returned from Sweden, at first as a labor reporter; but he soon became the paper's film critic, certainly an apolitical assignment.

He was not well paid at the *Daily News*, and the health problems of his two older daughters strained the Sandburg budget for many years. As early as 1920 he began to develop his lecture-recitals as an artistic endeavor and as a source of additional income to support his family. He had shown dramatic and oratorical abilities at Lombard College, and now in young middle age he found success on the stage. His programs combined readings of his poetry and fanciful stories for children, and the singing of folk songs and spirituals, interspersed with his own wry comments. His performances on college campuses and before civic and cultural groups were financially and critically successful. As a stage performer he rivaled Mark Twain and Will Rogers.

Throughout the early twenties Sandburg sought new outlets for his abilities—the stories for children, the biography for Lincoln, the stage performances, and the collecting of songs, published in 1927 as *The American Songbag*. Clearly he did not become a reactionary, but he repositioned himself in American society as poet and troubadour, storyteller, and biographer of a beloved, almost mythic president.

By the 1930s his role as cultural icon was fully established. He had returned to Lincoln studies in the late twenties, working on a four-volume biography of Lincoln as president. This was a mammoth project; the sources were voluminous, and Sandburg had no institutional support, no Guggenheim grant. He left the *Daily News* early in the depression, spending several months a year on the lecture circuit and devoting the rest of the year to research and writing. All through the thirties he labored away at a seemingly endless writing task he had set for himself.

In mid-decade he took time out to write his last major volume of poetry, the folksy work he called *The People, Yes*. This was his affirmation "of swarming and brawling Democracy[;] it attempts to give back to the people their own lingo."

In 1939 *Abraham Lincoln: The War Years* was at last published to great acclaim. It was a poetic interpretation, not a scholarly one, written for the general reader. Sandburg's reputation as a biographer was secure, and he received a Pulitzer Prize for history the following year. In 1951 he received the Pulitzer Prize for poetry. At the time his informal lecture-folksinging-poetry recitals were even more popular across the country. He and Robert Frost became the most applauded poet-performers in the land.

Sandburg published a few more poems in his old age; some of these poems were earlier works taken from what he called his "kit-bag" file. He appeared with symphonies to read Lincoln's words, and he made many radio and television appearances. In his performances, wherever they were, the poetry he read, his music, his witty comments—all were for the people.

Manuscripts of several hundred unpublished or uncollected Sandburg poems remain in the Sandburg Collection housed in the Rare Book and Special Collections Library of the University of Illinois at Urbana-Champaign. Many of these poems are from one of his best and strongest poetic periods, 1912–1922, his first decade as a journalist in Chicago. They show Sandburg as a critic of economic and social conditions in urban America; a walker in the city observing gritty street life, high life, and bohemian life; and a sensitive poet born to immigrant parents. He could record the cruelties of his society, the consequences of war, the despair of urban workers. He could write apolitical imagist poems and poems describing nature. He could also display a self-questioning, even romantic and tender side, especially in his ruminations and sometimes in some of his poems of protest, with their sympathetic identification with "the people."

Why didn't Sandburg publish these other hundreds of poems? In the "New Section" of his *Complete Poems* (1950), in *Harvest Poems* (1960), and in *Honey and Salt* (1963), he and his editors did make use of some poems in his vast backlog. Later in his life he may have deliberately excluded some of his early poems from a more radical time in his life. In some cases the poems may simply have been lost in the clutter of his files. At times he seems to have put poems aside for later revisions and then never returned to them. Some poems of his early period were unpublished at that time because of their language or subject matter or because he thought of them as workshop exercises.

We have attempted in this volume to make a representative selection from the unpublished or uncollected manuscripts available to us. We have grouped these poems into categories: Don MacGregor, Images and Colors, Chicago, Sense and Nonsense, An Indian Legend, Character Studies and Personalities, Protest Poems, Nature Poems, Literary and Movie Criticism, African-Americans, World War I, Ruminations, and Toward *The People, Yes.*

Sandburg prided himself on being a poet of the people, a poet who published simple poems for simple people. A few of the poems in this collection, however, are not easily understood without historical or literary explication, and that may be why Sandburg rejected them. When needed, we have attempted to provide necessary information for the context of the subject at the beginning of each section. Some of the poems we include do not demand such analysis, and we provide little or no comment on works clearly relating to Sandburg's "common people."

Most of the poems in this collection are from Sandburg's mature poetic period. He was an imaginative imagist and a believer in workers and their causes, a critic of those among the wealthy who were largely unconcerned about the economic and social fate of most Americans. At times he could be crude, especially but not exclusively in the first drafts of such poems as "Billy Sunday"; but his clear voice can be heard, and his compassion illuminates his calling as the poet of the people.

A NOTE ON THE TEXT

Obvious typographical errors in Sandburg's poems have been silently corrected.

Titles have been supplied for a few poems and are placed in brackets.

Some poems are dated by Sandburg, but most are not. We cannot now determine the exact date when the undated poems were written. In his "New Section" of *Complete Poems*, Sandburg himself left many of his poems undated.

The following poems have been lightly edited: "Terry Hut," "Socrates," "John James Audubon," "[He Sez / I Sez]," "[Henry James]," and "[Walt Whitman]."

Permission to publish the unpublished Sandburg poems has been granted by the Carl Sandburg Family Trust and the Library of the University of Illinois at Urbana-Champaign.

Don MacGregor

Don MacGregor was a "fair-haired Scotch boy with a soft heart, beautiful dreams and rare courage of both instinct and mind," Sandburg wrote Floyd Dell on December 5, 1929, long after MacGregor's death. Sandburg moved from Milwaukee to Chicago in September 1912 and worked at the Socialist newspaper, the *Chicago Evening World*, until it folded in December. When he joined *The Day Book* early in 1913, MacGregor was city editor. Floyd P. Gibbons wrote on April 12, 1916, in the *Chicago Tribune*, that the young Scottish-born newspaperman was well known in radical circles in Chicago: "His name was no strange one among the esoteric circles that form in Halsted street basements in the vicinity of Hull house or on North Clark Street, where one brings his own beer and occasionally contributes a quarter for the lagging gas meter." Sandburg was also drawn to these radical, somewhat bohemian circles.

Suffering from tuberculosis, MacGregor left Chicago sometime in 1913 for Colorado, where he did reporting for the *Denver Express*, a Scripps paper like *The Day Book*. In southern Colorado, miners were then trying to organize a union in the coal fields controlled by Rockefeller interests. When a strike was called for September 23, 1913, strikers were forced out of their company homes and into tent cities. MacGregor showed his idealism in his account of the strikers' migration to their new settlement. It was, he wrote in the *Express* on September 24, "an exodus of woe of a people leaving known fears for new terrors, a hopeless people seeking new hope, a people born to suffering going forth to new suffering." He counted fifty-seven wagons with strikers, their pitiful possessions, their blighted lives, and he described what he saw: "Little piles of miserable looking straw bedding! Little piles of kitchen utensils! And all so worn and badly used they would have been the scorn of any second-hand dealer on Larimer Street."

MacGregor wrote Sandburg on March 15, 1914, from Evergreen, Colorado, about the strikers: "They were so utterly pitiful, and it seemed so horrible that people did not understand how pitiful they were. The strikers were so vague and bewildered and lost-sheep-like in their striving after better things; the other side so beastly brutal, so unseeing, so certain they alone were right, and that the earth and the riches thereof were theirs by God-given right. It wasn't so much the actual instances of brutality that oppressed me; it was more this accursed incapability of the operators and those in power to see how utterly wrong they were, how brutal they were, and my own failure to make them see it.

"It was this that seems the saddest part of it all to me; for, after all, the operators and those in authority, here as elsewhere, are human beings, and they all must have consciences, and, since they have, and since they know they must sleep with themselves at night, they must pay some attention to the voices of these consciences. I always feel that if one could only get at men like that, get through the outer crust they use to repel all the thoughts they don't want to think, one might accomplish great things with them. But that is the hard thing to do, especially when preachers and scholars, sycophants of all degrees, are fawning upon them, and shouting to them that they are right, right, right, and that those who oppose them are anarchists and murderers."

MacGregor mentioned in this long letter that he had written half a dozen short stories while he was away from the labor strife. He noted, "I had no market for them, no assurance they would ever be published, that they ever would move anyone to pity for his brother."

He signed his emotional letter, "Yours until the hangman shall us part," a line Sandburg inserted into *The People, Yes*, with slight changes for poetic effect:

"Yours till the hangman doth us part,"
Don Magregor* ended his letters.

MacGregor wrote Sandburg again on April 12, just eight days before the brutal Ludlow Massacre in Colorado. During months of labor strife, Mother Jones had lent her presence to the cause of the strikers; Louis Tikas and other organizers in the union movement were opposed by the Colorado National Guard. On April 20 the Guard attacked the miners' tent city at Ludlow, burning the flimsy structures, senselessly killing women and children and strikers, including Tikas, the Greek-born labor leader. News of the massacre enraged liberals and radicals, and Sandburg obviously learned some of the awful details of death and destruction at Ludlow from newspaper accounts.

In his letter to Sandburg, MacGregor had no premonitions of the upcoming disaster, but he said he was no longer welcome at the *Denver Express* and wanted to return to *The Day Book* in Chicago, for "The Game is a bigger Game there, and it needs strong players."

But the Ludlow Massacre changed MacGregor's life. He immediately joined a group of eighty armed miners at Walsenburg, not far from Ludlow, where he became a guerrilla leader. Before a battle with the National Guard, MacGregor dressed himself in boots and bandoliers. When the

---

*Sandburg used the spellings MacGregor and Magregor.

battle was over both the strikers and the Guard had suffered casualties. MacGregor left the battlefield for Chicago, but soon, as leader of the strikers, he was indicted for murder by a Colorado grand jury.

The Ludlow Massacre stayed in the news. *The Day Book* on April 3, 1916, reported on "the revolt of Colorado miners against the Rockefeller iron hand in that state." Given all the excitement over this labor strife, it is possible, even likely, that Sandburg talked to MacGregor after his return to Chicago.

Sandburg wrote two poems about his fellow newsman. The first was "Don MacGregor's Curse," dated 1914, which captures the idealistic radical nature of his friend who castigates working-class people who do not fight their oppression, the oppressors themselves, and "all people satisfied." The refrain, "Damn 'em all, God," reflects MacGregor's revolutionary zeal that was reminiscent of the radical poet Percy Bysshe Shelley. Just when in 1914 the poem was written is unknown, but it was composed before the final phase of the young Scotsman's life began.

Fearing arrest because of the indictment in Colorado, MacGregor fled to Mexico, where Pancho Villa was leading a revolt against the Carranzo government. MacGregor continued as a reporter, often using the alias David Bruce. His sympathies were with the revolutionary Villa, but he was also aware that Villa had vowed death to gringos.

Floyd P. Gibbons, in Mexico as war correspondent for the *Chicago Tribune*, wrote about MacGregor's last hours, basing his story on the firsthand account of J. H. Locke. When Locke, MacGregor, and a German named Herman Blankenburg were in a hotel in Manaca, Mexico, site of a small Carranza garrison, Villa's forces overran the town. The three men knew they were in danger. Locke wanted to escape during the night, but Blankenburg refused, saying, "I am a German. I am not an American. Villa kills only Americans." MacGregor preferred to go with Locke but didn't wish to leave Blankenburg alone, so he stayed. Locke escaped but later learned what happened the next day, March 28, 1916, and offered this account to Gibbons:

At eight the next morning after Manaca was overrun, Blankenburg opened the door of the hotel, and as he walked into the street "a Villista officer, riding by at a gallop, drew up his horse and Blankenburg started to explain that he was not an American. His words were cut short by a blow from the officer's saber. The blade struck the German on the crown and split his skull in two. The Villista fired two shots into his body.

"Just then the officer saw MacGregor, who had started out to explain with his meager command of Spanish. He reached the sidewalk when the officer, unsheathing his rifle, sent two bullets through him. MacGregor dropped dead in the street.

"In the afternoon the pigs tried to eat the bodies, which still lay in the street. The Villistas were still in the town and the Mexicans were afraid to remove the bodies. But an old Mexican who is friendly to me sent his little boy over to the door of the hotel and the muchacho sat there through the day, throwing stones at the pigs to keep them away.

"In the morning the Villistas rode out of town and the bodies of MacGregor and Blankenburg, with those of eleven Carranzista soldiers, were carted to the edge of the town and buried in a common grave."

Sandburg read this account and turned the stories and legends about MacGregor into a poem called "Memoir of a Proud Boy," his second poem about his friend. The manuscript is not dated, but he sent a copy of it to Alice Corbin Henderson on June 29, 1917, indicating it was written just months after MacGregor's death.

Sandburg stayed close to the known facts as he described MacGregor's involvement in the Colorado mine strikes of 1913–1914. He drew upon MacGregor's two surviving letters to him, written in early 1914, on published newspaper accounts of the labor situation in Colorado and the Ludlow Massacre, and especially on Gibbons's account of MacGregor's death. But Sandburg mythologizes MacGregor's life and death in Mexico. It is certainly believable that the Scottish-born radical would have admired Villa, but it was a Villa officer who killed MacGregor, and it was the townspeople in Manaca who buried the reporter and the Carrazinistas slaughtered by Villa's forces.

In the poem Sandburg notes, "I would like to varnish the facts," and indeed he did. From his own perspective as a radical journalist and a friend of MacGregor, Sandburg wrote the end of the story the way MacGregor would have wanted it: the revolutionary is killed by reactionary forces and buried by radical forces.

Sandburg's published version of "Memoir of a Proud Boy" first appeared in *Cornhuskers* (1918). It is a moving elegy to his friend, but it does not contain the beginning and concluding lines of the version printed in this collection. As originally written, the beginning and ending contain many literary allusions. MacGregor's face is compared to that of Shelley; Sandburg clearly thought Shelley and MacGregor were revolutionaries who died too young. The "ashes of the heart" reference is perhaps to Shelley's cremation on the shore of the Italian coast: his heart refused to burn, and Edward John Trelawny reached into the rib cage and pulled out the heart. Sandburg clearly felt that Shelley's revolutionary zeal could not be consumed. Sandburg also says that the "ashes of the heart" remind him of one of his favorite writers—Stephen Crane, the daring war correspondent and sensitive writer of war stories and accounts of the down-

and-out of society in such novels as *Maggie: A Girl of the Streets*.

The opening and closing lines of the poem, with their literary references to Shelley and Crane, were perhaps omitted by Sandburg in his published version because he may have felt them too literary and thus inappropriate for a poem for the people.

Don MacGregor's Curse

Damn 'em all, God.
People who work all day in factories and stores for under
$10 a week and go on dying without ever having lived,
without a flash or a flicker of hate or a headlong love—
nothing but imitation clothes, words, thoughts and
wishes—without a fight or a sign of a fight in their $10
lives.

Damn 'em all, God.
People who live in glorious, rambling mansions satisfied to
fill their own bellies and go out every day and see
thousands and thousands of other people hungry and
living in shanties and slums.

Damn 'em all, God.
All people satisfied, all people who've got all they want, all
people afraid of storms and war, all people fixed and
easy, ready for the end of a world that never will end.

Damn 'em all, God.

[1914]

30

Memoir of a Proud Boy

Don Magregor had a face like Shelley
For those who remember Shelley's face.

West wind and cloud, in western places,
Wrote on his face the same . . . quizzicalities.

He lived on the wings of storm and so died.
The ashes of his heart look to me like Stevie Crane.

Out of Ludlow and Walsenburg and Trinidad in Colorado
Sprang a vengeance of Croatian miners, Italians, Scots.
And the killings ran under spoken commands of this boy.
They killed red-handed remembering the shot and charred
Wives and children of Ludlow, remembering Louis Tikas,
The Greek . . . a skull cracked by a rifle butt . . .
The death of a laughing blue-eyed man from Athens
Doubly ensured with a bullet and a rifle butt.

As a splash of red endeavor
It held the nation a week
And one or two million men stood together
And swore by the retribution of steel.

It was all accidental.
He lived flecking lint off coat lapels
Of men he talked with,
And he kissed the miners' babies
And wrote a Denver paper
Of picket silhouettes on a mountain line.

He had no mother but Mother Jones
Crying from a jail window of Trinidad:
"All I want is room enough to stand
And shake my fist at the enemies of the human race."

Named by a grand jury as a murderer
He went to Chihuahua, forgot his old Scotch name,
And smoked cheroots with Pancho Villa
And wrote home of Villa as a rock of the people.

How can I tell how Don Magregor went?

Three riders emptied lead into him
And he lay on the main street of an inland town
And a boy sat near all day throwing stones
To keep wandering pigs away.

The Villa men buried him in a pit
With twenty Carranzistas dead from Villa bullets.

There is drama in that point . . .

About the boy and the pigs.
Griffith would make a movie of it to fetch sobs.
Victor Herbert would have the drums whirr in a weave
With a high fiddlestring's single clamor.

"And the muchacho sat there all day throwing stones
To keep the pigs away," wrote Gibbons to the Tribune.
Maybe embellishments are wanted.
It doesn't run like a Poe shudder story.
Maybe the blood of it is too warm.

I would like to varnish the facts
And make the kaleidoscopic quizotry of it
Quiver with what the sea guesses at the moon.

Somewhere in Chihuahua or Colorado
Is a suitcase full of poems and short stories.
. . . brave, red-blooded writing
. . . junk.

This is enough:
He had a face like Shelley
For those who remember Shelley's face.
The ashes of his heart look to me like Stevie Crane.

Images and Colors

Sandburg was influenced by the Imagist movement, with its indebtedness to Japanese and Chinese poetry and to the French Symbolists. Imagism, a movement in modern poetry strongest during the years 1909–1917, was led by Ezra Pound and Amy Lowell. The Imagists used precise images, free verse, and avoided the stilted vocabulary of the Victorians. Sandburg wrote in the Imagist tradition at times, but his poems of social and economic protest were numerous. His friend Amy Lowell had many reservations about his protest poems, calling them propagandistic. She kept encouraging him to concentrate more on his Imagist works. Sandburg did not ignore Lowell's views, and some of his best-known poems—including "Fog"—are pure images, without social or political context. The poems in this section begin with "Moon Dance," "Sunday," and "Wings," all three filled with colors and vivid imagery.

Again influenced by Amy Lowell, Sandburg during his early years in Chicago was interested in Chinese poetry and paintings. In his "Li Po and Lao Tse Come to Nebraska," he combines Taoist imagery with the economic concerns of Nebraska farmers. The juxtaposition of Chinese image and Nebraska farming is particularly striking in a poem that contains radical social and economic undertones.

The last poem in this section, "Fire Flowers," dated 1920, was published in the *New Republic* of March 23, 1932, but has never been collected. As John Hallwas has perceptively observed, the poem "clearly contrasts two characteristic aspects of the poet's consciousness: his awareness of the plight and struggle of American working men, and his ability to see delicate beauty . . . in smokestacks." The colors and shapes spewing from the smokestacks—the "flowers of fire," the "purple flames," the "glass roses"—are vivid images indeed when overlaid with the scornful words of workers still waiting for their promised eight-hour day. Their grammar is far from perfect, but the sense of their disenchantment is real, so real that when, at the end of the poem, Sandburg concludes "such language," the reader knows, with Sandburg and the workers, that the language of image and beauty is insufficient to the magnitude of economic reality. In this fine poem it appears that Amy Lowell's literary influence on Sandburg had weakened. He had chosen instead his much stronger voice of propaganda and social protest.

Moon Dance

Birch-white streaks moon-white in Wisconsin.
Red November leaves call the graves of Red Indian girls.
The moon dance of the birches is done to the regular
  monotonous strumming of the wind in the leaves.

Sunday 9|26

Bells of Sunday in September
Clanged across the roofs
Calling all the little people.
    In my garden *or garen upon*
Where the purple petals wavered
I remember yellow aster masses
Sagging under a slow soft wind.
A yellow-bellied bumblebee
Buzzed around a red, red dragon.

[1910]

Wings

"My frail body cannot hold its great moods."

Fat pigeons in the railroad freight yard
Are eating wheat grains spilled among the cinders.
One with blue wings dappled darkly picks faster than any
    other.
By the shuttling of his neck and mouth
    He passes all in the rapid grabbing of the grain.

His belly curves to a swollen paunch
And he waddles with eye keen and mouth swift.
I swear I saw this fat pigeon fail in flying, swing his wings in
    useless flapping,
Held among the cinders while a lean grey gull shot silent
    and lonesome in a straight line toward the river and the
    red sunset and one yellow star.

Li Po and Lao Tse Come to Nebraska

1.
Make a daily memo of your eggs.
Give up something you love to get something better to love.
Throw away your last hope rather than undersell.

2.
Loosen a sprig of cherry blossom
    and see how it smells.
Break off a line of lilacs long
    as your arm.

3.
Stage your fat steers for the butcher's eye
Stand at a hog-tight fence and count your hams,
Reckon on the sagging corn-fed flanks.

Fire Flowers

Flowers of fire bloom as grand poppy leaves reaching and
eager out of the smokestacks of Gary.

*(What about that eight-hour day they was telling us
about?)*

The sprockets of purple flame, blazing their criss-cross
pictures on the black print of the night are pretty, so pretty.

*(That was a lot of hooey about the eight-hour day, wasn't
it?)*

The fire streaks up into the sky and breaks—it is thousands
of glass roses spreading and shattering off into the black
bowl of the sky up over.

(Sure we got the eight-hour day—like hell.)

Here's a fire-white vase holding green stalks of fire—it melts
into crying chrysanthemums—it fades to a heave of rolling
smoke.

*(You needn't say I said so but what they told us about
that eight-hour day was just a plain goddam lie.)*

Ai! ai! the fire colors rise in the evening—such oranges the
smoke shovels! such bananas on black shoulders! such
alphabets of flame! such mushrooms of gold and pearl!
such lavender ladders of smoke talk! such language!

[1920]

Chicago

Most of Sandburg's best poems about Chicago were written while he was a journalist at *The Day Book* and the *Daily News*. He told his first biographer, Karl Detzer, that during this early period of his life in the city (*The Day Book* days, especially), "I would write a poem a day, keeping a sort of free-verse journal." Certainly there is a quality of freshness, of life observed and captured, of language real and spoken, of slang not now politically correct ("wop") in some of these poems. In many of them, also, as John E. Hallwas has noted in his Introduction to *Chicago Poems*, Sandburg was at this period of his life concerned for the oppressed workers he saw all around him, workers "being subverted by a wealthy group that has established an economic system based on . . . exploitation. . . ." That is certainly the case in "[Two-Dollars-a-Day Wop]." The exhausted Italian-born laborer is old and tired after a twelve-hour day, too tired to repeat, "What about that eight-hour day they was telling us about?"

In "Crayon" Sandburg offers a touching sketch of a girl from a poor family who, on her way to work, reads about a society lady who wore a choker of pearls. The poor girl could not imagine what a "dog collar of pearls" might be. The gulf between poverty and wealth is unbridgeable. The pearl-laden wealthy lady is probably Mrs. Potter Palmer, a frequent target of Sandburg's scorn. She was often photographed wearing her "dog collar of pearls." The young girl is one of the thousands Sandburg saw daily on the streets of Chicago.

In "[Wilderness Man]" Sandburg is an observer of the old frontier man who has become one of the down-and-out in Chicago, his wilderness qualities destroyed in the industrial world. Sandburg does not know the whiskered man, does not interview him, but sees him vividly:

I saw the smut of the city on the wilderness.
I say here's a wolf turned alley dog.

In "Speed Bug" Sandburg turns to the middle-class exploiters in the city. A man whose careless driving had killed one person and crippled two used his lawyers effectively to avoid paying any personal injury costs. When this building contractor was himself killed by an interurban train, some religious people looked upon his death as "retribution" and "an act of God." Sandburg, the reporter, sees a different view: "Others left God out of the case and said they were glad the Aurora and Elgin motorman on that interurban car felt like making high speed that morning." The poem reflects not only the violence typically reported in newspapers (the contractor was disemboweled) but also the disaffection of the people of the city, their satisfaction when the well-to-do who can pervert justice with their expensive lawyers get their own comeuppance.

"Selling Spiel [on Maxwell Street]" is an unadorned picture of life on Maxwell Street on the Near West Side of Chicago. Sandburg the neutral observer hears the exaggerations of the street vendor's slice-of-selling spiel. Sandburg the poet-reporter sees without comment the blanket with blood spots "woven into it by design."

"Good Woman" is one of Sandburg's reporter-poems about the dense James Aloysius McGillicuddy who killed his wife and didn't understand why. Sandburg perhaps interviewed the killer at the county jail or read about the perplexed McGillicuddy in one of the local newspapers. In this poem Sandburg again gives an account of urban life without added comment. The language of the murdered woman, as reported by the Irish husband, is poetic and tragic, qualities Sandburg often expressed in these Chicago poems.

"Now You Take Her" appears to be a love poem of the *Chicago Poems* period, told by a disillusioned lover who spent his money on a gold digger and now, money gone, is ready to pass her on to someone who can afford her.

"Bonbons" is a return to the slang-filled Chicago days and to love that can be bought with expensive candies. Sandburg knew the cynical urban views about love expressed in this poem, but he himself was oftentimes a romantic.

We believe that "The Lower Register" was inspired by a line in Walt Whitman's *Song of Myself*: "The pure contralto sings in the organ loft." We have included Whitman's line as a rubric to Sandburg's poem. In Sandburg's version a disturbed woman sits at the end of the pier holding red flowers, perhaps reflecting a passionate relationship. She shreds the flowers, says "God" and "something else" to herself. She goes to the Episcopal church and sings expressively in the choir, but what troubles her? A faithless lover? A friend's betrayal? The poem suggests mystery, gives no answers, but the woman's voice moves the Episcopal worshipers—and the reader.

"Studio Saturday Afternoon" is probably a reflection of another aspect of Sandburg's early years in Chicago. During his work as a reporter on *The Day Book* he met Edgar Lee Masters, and the two men made excursions into the artistic, bohemian world of Chicago that in 1914 Masters knew little about. As Masters wrote in his autobiography, *Across Spoon River*, "The town had studios where there were painters and sculptors, and it had the precursors of the flappers, and here and there men and women were living together in freedom, just as they did in Paris." Sandburg talked to his first biographer about writers who "hung batik curtains in the windows of converted coach houses in alleys behind the Gold Coast 'castles' and went in for 'atmosphere.'" "Studio Saturday Afternoon" is Sandburg's passionless report on the conversations of three "artistic" young women in a studio. The women are static, they do not come and go speaking of Michelangelo as they do in "The Love Song of J. Alfred Prufrock." Their conversations are more personal, discursive, and vapid.

In "A Long Shot" Sandburg, amusing himself and his readers, passes on the predictions of a gypsy fortune-teller. In "Young Woman" he writes admiringly of another gypsy fortune-teller, a woman who is free and easy, attractive to men, a wanderer, a passionate lover. The poet knows that she has multitudes of stories to tell, but he does not approach her. He has only an easy admiration for her and her life.

"Sandburg to Loeb" was published in *The Day Book* on September 8, 1915, but never collected by Sandburg. It is a difficult poem to read, especially after the Holocaust, for the central character, a villain, is Jewish. At the heart of the poem is the effort of Jacob Loeb, businessman and member of the Chicago Board of Education, to break the Chicago Teachers' Federation, led by Margaret Haley, a friend of Sandburg's. The Federation had joined the Chicago Federation of Labor. The so-called Loeb Rule, passed by the Board of Education on September 1, 1915, "prohibited teachers from belonging to organizations affiliated with organized labor or employing paid business representatives."

Just days before the anti-union rule was passed, Loeb had refused to allow the Hebrew Institute to sponsor a meeting organized by the Labor Defense League to raise money for "union labor men who are unjustly held in prison." About five hundred students, most of them Russian

Jews attending the Institute to study English, went on strike "to gain freedom of speech."

The Day Book published many reports about Loeb and his vendetta against the teachers' union and against free speech. It had also reported on the death on August 17 of Leo Frank, a Jew lynched in Georgia. That same day in 1915, Kovno, now in Lithuania, fell to the German army, and the press began to publish stories about the atrocities of the retreating Russian army against the Jews of that area. In addressing the American-born Loeb, Sandburg writes, "You came from Kovno," in an attempt to identify Loeb "with the repressions of Europe."

"Sandburg to Loeb" is a slashingly polemical work and extremely difficult for modern readers to consider dispassionately. There is no indication in Sandburg's life and work that he was anti-Semitic, but this bold poem is likely to be misinterpreted. It has been reprinted twice in recent years by Robert L. Reid and is included here because it reflects an aspect of Sandburg's radicalism during his *Day Book* years. His sympathies here, as always during his radical years, are with those fighting repression.

[Two-Dollars-a-Day Wop]

A two-dollars-a-day wop sits in the corner of the streetcar
Dozing in a half stupor at the end of a twelve-hour day.
    Across his face run wrinkles
    Of a grizzled old-timer:
Count the years on his arms and legs and he is a young
    man,
Look at his face and he is half ready for the grave.
He is an old-timer but not in years.

                  [1915]

Crayon

The sewer digger's daughter hears her mother say
    the family will have eggs for breakfast when
    eggs are easier to get.
And the daughter riding with her hand in a strap on
    a trolley car, going to her job in a corset factory,
Reads a morning newspaper society page twice and is
    teased all day by thought of what a "dog collar of
    pearls" might be.

[1913]

[Wilderness Man]

Whiskers a wren could nest in.
Cheekbones with an inlay of sun tan.
Shrewd eyes . . . ox shoulders . . .
He passed us in the rain tonight
Among the ragtags of South State Street
And he had a big red umbrella keeping off the rain
And a gunny sack under his left arm.

I could understand the old wilderness man
And the wish of his heart for a spot of red
In the mass of dark umbrellas
And I don't care what he had in the gunny sack.
Kittens, pups, bread scraps—I don't care.
But why did he rush along like a city-broke
        newspaper delivery horse?
Why did he walk furiously like a messenger boy
        after a tip or detectives going to make a raid?

I saw the smut of the city on the wilderness.

I said here's a wolf turned alley dog.

Speed Bug

Edward Singleton ran his motor car into four people, two of
them children, at various times in his career of rushing
from job to job as a building contractor.

One died and two were crippled for life and Singleton
appealed the personal injury suits to the higher courts
and told his lawyers to keep the litigants busy spending
money carrying the cases to higher courts.

When the Aurora and Elgin interurban car smashed into
Singleton's car one day in a suburb and not only killed
Singleton but disemboweled him forty feet along the
tracks,

There were some good church folks said it was retribution
and an act of God.

Others left God out of the case and said they were glad the
Aurora and Elgin motorman on that interurban car felt
like making high speed that morning.

Selling Spiel [on Maxwell Street]

This blanket is a tough weave, sir.
Those blood spots were woven into it by design.   *ground*
The yarns were chosen from sheep and goats tried by zero
    weather, blizzards, undiminishing wind and hard usage.
You will not wear out this blanket in your lifetime, sir, nor
    mine.
The weaving was done slowly; they took their time, sir; they
    were stubborn about the materials; just one of those
    accidental-looking blood spots took ten years, sir.

Good Woman

When James Aloysius McGillicuddy
had killed the woman he loved
and refused to talk about it
he found himself making explanations
to himself:
>"She could change herself *by Bran*
>into a bubble for me to play with.
>'I'll be your bubble' she says to me
>'kiss me   kick me   kill me
>break me like a big rainbow bubble
>I shall be light for you
>light as a lingering loving bubble
>take me   throw me   handle me with care
>or finger me like a fool *3rd finge Marcus*
>and see me vanish before your eyes.'"

And after thus quoting the woman he had killed
James Aloysius McGillicuddy began wondering to himself
whether she had talked like that   so fierce   so funny
whether he was imagining things   after the excitement
of sending a slug of lead into a woman's bosom and yet
he swore to himself:
>"She was a bubble   she told me
>she was a bubble   made for me
>and nobody else   and I could
>make her or break her
>   and why the hell I broke her
>I dont know
>   she was a goddam good woman
>I dont know why it happened
>she was such a goddam good woman"

Now You Take Her

You take her; I don't want her.
You brag her beauty; you pay for
    her clothes and bonbons and
    vanity bags; I'm through.
I took a pleasure in the contrast
    she made with scrawny women who
    were afraid of love; I bought her
    everything she wanted so long
    as my money lasted; now you take
    her.

Bonbons

Perhaps you also have passed show windows
And seen boxes of bonbons at $50 a throw,
Two bits apiece for chocolates,
Each one of the chocolates wrapped by itself
With its individuality protected like an Indian papoose,
Guarded and distinguished for a lady's mouth,
Each separate bonbon almost demanding a nurse and a
    policeman to watch it.
Perhaps you too have ejaculated:
    This is the candy to send women who are won by
    candy.

The Lower Register

["The pure contralto sings in the organ loft."
—Walt Whitman, *Song of Myself*]

A woman sits
On the end of the pier
Sunday morning,
Her legs crossed,
A handful of red flowers
In her right fist.

She watches
Now the muddy gray
Of water nearby,
Now the far blue
And fading lavender
Where sky meets sea
At the harbor edge.
    She loosens petals
    In twos and threes
    And drops them slowly
    In the muddy gray
    Swashing the posts
    Of the pier.

She says "God" to herself
    and something else
And then walks down to the Episcopal church
    and sings in the choir.

The worshipers gossip about her wonderful contralto voice,
How the sob of it searches out the farthest benches and
    corners of the church.

Studio Saturday Afternoon

Three young women in V's studio on a Saturday afternoon.

V   tantalizes the ivories furbishing her impressions of
a concert tour of Texas, favorable critical notices in
Dallas newspapers, and a drawling cowboy who told her
he knew nothing about art but enjoyed music and "could
love a woman if he had a chance."

L   sings Mexican folk songs never published, gathered
firsthand when she lived as a girl near Tampico, slept
on the ground in the wilderness, and learned a piece
fathers croon to their daughters-in-arms, as to say:
"You are barefooted now but they sell shoes at the
gates of Heaven."

J   sits a cool image cross-legged on a couch smoking a
cigaret, discursive of love, and how a blond real estate
man who called on her three times in one week following
the Art Institute masquerade ball, never shows up any more.

A Long Shot

A half-dollar in the hands of a gypsy
    tells this:

You shall go broken on the wheel,
    lashed to the bars and fates of steel,
    a nickel's worth of nothing,
        a vaudeville gag,
    a child's busted rubber balloon kicked
        amid dirty bunting and empty popcorn
        bags at a summer park.

Yet cigarmakers shall name Havanas for you and
    paste your picture on the box.

Racehorses foaming under scarlet and yellow-shirted
    jockeys shall wear your name.

And policemen direct strangers to parks and schools
    remembered after you.

Young Woman

You are a Halsted Street gypsy running a shop
Where shovelmen pay fifty cents apiece to hear you tell
The luck of their lives waiting for them on the long rough
    road.
You call them with signs and symbols painted in crosses
    and black cats on the front door of your place.
Now you sit in a smoker on the elevated across the aisle
    from me
And you throw your right foot under your left knee and go
    on talking with your mother.
Men looking on don't bother you; the steady run of short
    musical words keeps coming from your lips.

On your face I read prairie sunrises and mountain dawns,
    horses, wagons, campfires, and men with high
    cheekbones and few words to strangers.
In your eyes are escapes; under your lashes is the dark and
    deep of a coal pit when the miners rise from the mouth
    at evening with lamps stuck on their caps.
On your cheeks is the shine of honeymoon linen—the clean
    breathing of early daylight—and the low whistling of
    dances in the wet grass—and the finding of a spring
    where clear water and gravel speak psalms and the call
    is for drinking with cupped hands.

How many men have sworn to forget your face and
    remembered? When will knives come into the story,
    handles dabbed with red thumbs? Who of the tribe will
    take you and let you be stolen?
Gypsy across from me in the smoker of an elevated car,
    blathering to your mother in a run of short words, you

with your right foot under your left knee, you are a
  whole row of story books.
I get off at State and Dearborn; you get off somewhere else;
  I wish you luck; love and love will hammer you; I wish
  you luck.

Sandburg to Loeb

To Jacob M. Loeb:
  You are one of the Jews sore at Georgia for the way
they hanged Leo Frank and called him a damned Jew there
in Atlanta.
  And you're talking a lot about liberty and the rights of
school children.
  You came from Kovno in Russia and you ought to
know something about liberty;
  And how school boards, police boards, military boards
and czars have gone on year after year
  To choke the Jews from having societies, organizations,
labor unions,
  Shoving bayonets into the faces of the Jews and driving
them to the ghettoes.
  You know what I mean. You know these European
cities where they call the Jews a despised race;
  And anybody who spits in a Jew's face is not touched
by the police.
  D'ye get me? I'm reminding you what you already
know.
  You're the man who is leading the school board fight
on the Teachers' Federation.
  And you forget, your memory slips, your heart doesn't
picture
  How you and your fathers were spit upon in the face.
  And how the soldiers and police misused your
women—
  Just because they were Jews, and in Kovno
  Anybody could get away with what they did to a Jew
woman or a Jew girl;

And now you, a Jew, stand up here in Chicago and act proud

Because you have in effect spit in the faces of Chicago women, accused them, belittled them.

First you tried to cut their wages, back here in May, a seven-and-a-half per cent cut,

And now you're going to make it a law that teachers can't have a labor union;

And they got to take what you and Rothmann and Myer Stein hand 'em.

I don't think you'll get away with it.

Sam Gompers, an English Jew, will speak tonight at the Auditorium,

And Jacob LeBosky and Sam Alschuler and other Jews in this town

Are against the game of shackling the teachers and repeating Kovno and Kiev and Odessa here in Chicago.

In fact, five hundred Jews are already in revolt at your Kovno trick

Of slamming the door on free speech at the Hebrew Institute.

These five hundred are the real blood of the Jew race

That give it a clean flame of heroism.

You belong with the trash of history, the oppressors and the killjoys.

[1915]

Sense and Nonsense

The stream-of-consciousness thoughts of the heavy man in "The Fleas of Flanders" are comic, tragic, nonsensical. The heavy man does not think of the bloody battles fought in Flanders during World War I. Fleas and flannels trivialize Flanders, making nonsense of battles that were too horrible to contemplate. The fleas, of course, were afflictions of the soldiers in the trenches. In his wandering mind, the heavy man thinks about headlines of a woman murdering a man, then transforms his disturbing thoughts into one-liners. He invents a story of a death-row inmate turning handsprings on the way to the electric chair: death and fleas and Flanders and their sounds come to his mind, but the real meaning of Flanders eludes him. He slides into thoughts of marriage and murder with Flanders hovering over all at the edge of his consciousness.

"The Pie-Wagon Driver" is set on the moon, though the language of the driver is mostly earthbound. His pies (round like the moon) are typically American, and the children have moon faces. They are abbadabba children with abba-dabba talk. Sandburg was drawing on the 1914 novelty song "Aba Daba Honeymoon," with its "aba daba" chimpanzee chatter and its catchy refrain:

"Ab-a, dab-a, dab-a, dab-a, dab-a, dab-a dab,"
Said the Chim-pie to the Monk,—
"Bab-a, dab-a, dab-a, dab-a, dab-a, dab-a, dab,"
Said the Mon-key to the Chimp.—
All night long they'd chat-ter a-way,
All day long they were hap-py and gay,
Swing-ing and sing-ing in their hun-ky ton-key way.

Sandburg had undoubtedly heard the song, but perhaps he had never seen the sheet music. His spelling of abbadabba is erratic, as is often the case in his nonsense poems, but the chatter of children around the pie wagon is quite effective for the reader's entertainment.

This section ends with "[Lullaby]." Sandburg told Norman Corwin, then preparing *The World of Carl Sandburg*: "I tried to make verbal music in this one. To some people it borders on the silly. In a certain sense, relaxation comes with the right kind of silliness."

The Fleas of Flanders

Do the fleas of Flanders wear flannels?
Thus a heavy man was asking.
His heart was heavy, his head heavy.
Heavy heavy hangs over: he kept saying.
What was he to the fleas of Flanders
And why should he think of them in flannels?
The answer, no, the answer couldn't be found
In a statement on the origin of fleas.
In a pragmatic consideration of Flanders,
And a history of the use of flannels.
His heart was heavy, his head heavy.
He read bulletins from the bedside of a dying man.
He filled a notebook with talk of people.
"She never loved him or she wouldn't have killed him."
"She did too love him or she couldn't have killed him."
"She was a cheap floozy, if you want my opinion."
"Don't ask me, I ain't no mind reader."
"The hell of it is she didn't have no mind to read."
"Now take me I wouldn't never have married her."
"Yes you know a hell of a lot about who you'd marry."
He read more bulletins about the dying man.
Not yet was the man dead; the affair dragged.
He decided to forget the dying man.
He would let the newspapers worry.
He thanked the newspapers, however, for a story.
A man walked out of the death house at Sing Sing
Saying to himself, Laugh clown laugh.
And suddenly seeing the electric chair
The man turned a couple of handsprings
And walked on his hands to the chair.
Here was a man who was ready.

71

Of how many of the teeming millions over the earth
Could it be said, He was ready for his big moment?
Though dead now he too undoubtedly had his thoughts
Of whether fleas in Flanders wear flannels.
He too perhaps had wondered whether he would marry
And if so which woman he would pick
And if so whether she could kill him for love
And if so whether he could read her deepest thoughts.
Sometimes thoughts run out of holes like rats.
Sometimes they chase each other like dogs and cats.
Sometimes they stand still like frost at dawn.
Sometimes they arch with the slow white suspensions
Of the silver prisms of the aurora borealis.

The Pie-Wagon Driver

Once I was a pie-wagon driver
sitting with pies piled high
to the right, to the left,
peach, apple, huckleberry,
up over, down under, behind me
lemon, cream, whiffleberry,
oriole, magnolia, whiffenspoof,
short hot pies, slow cool pies.
Long ago on streets of the moon
it was me driving a pie-wagon,
me me me among many many pies.
Moon children came to see me
laughing at me with moon faces
and I sold them moon-pies
a nickel apiece, a penny apiece.
They said thank you thonk you
mister mister thank you thonk you
I said think you thank me
      think you thonk me
as I sold them moon pies
a nice new nickel apiece
a purty purty penny apiece.
And had I smooth abbadabba pies
for the smooth abbadabba children?
Had I? Did I? I had. I did.
And each of them took two pies,
one to eat on, one to sit on,
sometimes two to eat, two to sit on,
always talking their abbadabba talk
      calling their abbadabba calls,

one asking the others, "Abbadabba?"
and the others answering together,
"You, me, us, every one of us,
    abbadabba, all abbadabba!"

[Lullaby]

Come to me dreaminess
come to me soon and see me
go sleep go slip go slag
come down oh dreaminess
come falling slow
come falling long and slow
now when the leaves are falling
now in the falltime moon
come springerly sprangerly sprong
come desta podesta dreaminess
now at the fall of leaves
now in the falltime moon

An Indian Legend

When Sandburg was helping Norman Corwin prepare the text for *The World of Carl Sandburg*, he had this comment about "[Pass This Baby On]":

"As a boy I attended a series of performances—admission free—of the Kickapoo Indians. . . . They sold Sagwa, a tonic, that was supposed to cure general lassitude. . . . There was nothing in what these Kickapoos did that was at all connected with the noble Indian spirit of this poem. When I wrote it I had been under the influence of a translation of Indian songs and poems by Frances Densmore, a woman who lived in Red Wing, Minnesota, and who had been adopted into several Indian tribes. Also around that time I went through books of Indian lore, and was struck by this legend in particular. It blesses the helpless until they get their start."

Sandburg also told Corwin that "I was influenced by Indian poems while writing 'Chicago.'"

The manuscript of "[Pass This Baby On]" was given to Norman Corwin to be used as a text in the play, and is not found in the Sandburg Collection at the University of Illinois.

[Pass This Baby On]

Can you make baby poems
For those who love special babies—
    clean antiseptic babies?
What of those Red Indian babies
fresh from the birthing-crotch?
For each of them the mystery-man raised
his right hand toward the sky and called:
"Hey you sun moon stars
    and you winds clouds rain mist,
    "Listen to me! listen!
"The news is another baby belonging
    has come to this earth of ours.
"Make its path smooth so it can reach
    the top of the first hill
    and the second hill.
"And hey you valleys rivers lakes trees grasses
you make its path smooth so it can reach
    the top of the third hill.
    "And listen you birds of the air,
    you animals of the tall timbers,
    you bugs and creepers
    you too listen!
"All you of sky earth and air, I ask you, beg you
"Pass this baby on till it climbs up over
    and beyond the fourth hill.
"From then on this child will be strong enough
"To travel on its own and see what is beyond
    these four hills!"

Character Studies and
Personalities

Sandburg was an admirer of Edgar Lee Masters's *Spoon River Anthology*, and he too wrote a series of character and personality sketches. But Sandburg did not, as Masters did, return to recollections of his early days in small-town America; instead he worked almost entirely with historic figures, mostly American, though he reached as far back as Socrates. Also unlike Masters, he was not drawn to Freudian interpretations. At times Sandburg could be wryly comic in his sketches, as in his depiction of an unnamed Indiana farmer in "Terry Hut," who swears damnation on Terre Haute when his daughter runs into sexual misadventure in that city.

A few of these poems, especially "Daniel Boone" and "[Davvy Tipton]," might well have been included in *The People, Yes* as part of the panorama of American life.

The last poem in the section, "Iron Jaw," is not about any particular American Puritan divine, such as Jonathan Edwards or Cotton Mather. It is about Pilgrim fathers who knew how to recognize evil and who knew that sinners would surely die. If Sandburg had any quarrel with religion, it was with "four-flushers" like Billy Sunday and self-proclaimed arbiters of human behavior. Not surprisingly then, the bigoted Pilgrim father in "Iron Jaw" is treated with Sandburgian scorn.

Terry Hut

An old Indiana farmer
With much money and a hatchet face
Used to squirt tobacco juice
And swear at Terry Hut.
His daughter went to a church carnival there
And a salesman from a buggy factory in South Bend
Who was brought to the feet of Jesus by Billy Sunday
In the famous revival in Philadelphia,
Got the farmer's daughter in the family way.
     Now even though Gene Debs
And some of God's shining lights are in that city,
The old farmer squirts tobacco juice and swears damnation
On Terry Hut as the dirtiest hole of a town in the world.

Daniel Boone

The Indians plucked out all his hair except a tuft on the
crown of the head dressed out with feathers and
ribbons.
They gave him a river water baptism to cleanse him of white
blood.
Blackfish, the chief of the Shawanese, painted his face and
spoke ancient rituals transforming him from a white to
a red man.

And yet, as he himself said, he "departed in a most secret
manner," and warned Boonsborough the Indians were
coming.

This was not the last time the red man tried to make a red
man of him.
He knew the alphabets of wind and weather, the tricks of
making fire in rain; he could read the footprints of men,
deer, bear, buffalo, and had killed of each of them.
So this was not the last time the red men said, "Under his
white skin he is red like us."

When he died they found he had his coffin, made with his
own hands, ready under his bed for the last long sleep.
He was eighty-two and was laid alongside his wife who died
seven years before him.
Of what rough travel and hard going in the next world can
these two be afraid?

Theodosia Burr

She was her father's daughter till the end.
When a child she learned to read Latin poetry and to speak
French and to seek knowledge; it was her father who
taught her, who told her personal charm was the first
gift; and for her, always, her father held the miracles of
knowledge and charm.
When her son was born she knew her father was to be head
of a great Western empire, if all went well, and her son
was to be heir to the throne, if all went well.
When her father was tried for treason at Richmond, she
stood by, she wrote letters, begged, conjured, and he
went free.
Again when he was an outlaw and an exile in England she
stood by, wrote letters, and made a way for him to
come back to the homeland.

And did his heart freeze, on landing in Boston, to hear how
now her son ran on phantom feet, the boy who should
have been heir to an empire, if all had gone well?
Again, did his heart freeze at the word of her on the pilot-
boat "Patriot," foundering in a storm and vanishing
into the mist wraiths of the clamorous Atlantic ocean?
Did the heart of Aaron Burr freeze? We do not know.
We only know she was his daughter to the end.

Alice and Phoebe Cary

In their book of poems two in three were written by Alice,
    one in three by Phoebe; Alice was invalid, Phoebe did
    the housework.
Their words reached homes from the Atlantic to the
    Mississippi; pioneers, frontiersmen, and California
    forty-niners read their pages; yet as children a
    stepmother would not allow them candles to read by.
They kept open house in New York City every Sunday night
    for fifteen years.
"Nearer Home," from Phoebe's pen, sings of "one sweetly
    solemn thought," which was a gift.

Elbert Hubbard

The great maker of failures came to a successful man.
Fifty volumes of epigrams, prophecies, and sermons were
    useless when the ship sunk.
The great man who spoke "I" loudly many years
Was swept into the vast suckhole of the sea
Along with deck hands, stokers, waiters, and
    chambermaids.
There is a great maker of failures who listens to no chatter
    from the American businessman when it's time to die.
You can't slip any money to Death and put it over.

Death listens to no go-betweens.
Death is an honest man.

[Davvy Tipton]

Davvy Tipton began on flatboats on the Ohio River.
Packets, towboats, snagboats, excursion boats, later he
    knew them as horsemen know horses.
The feel of the freshwater currents was a feel good to his
    feet.
He sat in pilot houses roaming the Ohio, the Mississippi,
    the Missouri: he knew the Mississippi from St. Paul to
    the Gulf; the Rock Island rapids, the Des Moines
    rapids, were the dirty pages of a much-read book for
    him; he knew their ins and outs.
If he weighed three hundred pounds and took up all the
    spare room in the little pilot houses—what of it?
Let big rivers have big men.
He swore and no woman ever heard him.
He swore and men thought afterward about his oaths.

He was a baby on the Muskingum River in 1828, a
    freshwater baby; he died sitting in the pilot house of the
    General A. Mackensie, under way in Lake Pepin in
    1904.

He died at the wheel
and they named the boat the *David Tipton*
and buried him at Rock Island.

No wife nor kin mourned him.
Along many rivers they said, "Davy Tip's gone on the
    longest river of all, to join his dog, Tobey Tip."

Socrates

I know Socrates was ridiculous, Jack,
And nobody in Athens who was anybody
Let it be known they knew him.

Snub nose, bald head, bare feet,
He never had any holeproof sox,
He never had his hair singed by a barber,
And he was the despair of dermatologists
Who make over the faces God gives men and women.

Went around Athens asking questions, Jack
All kinds of questions, Old Socrates,
Put straight to all kinds of people
Because he wasn't particular:
Lawyer, banker, policeman, street woman,
He asked them why they are here
Who we all are and where we are going all.

I know Socrates was ridiculous, Jack
Telling the men who ran Athens
He knew God and death and government
Down to fine points as well as they,
Down to the darkest deepest points
He claimed he had the dope as sure as they.

    O yes, I know,
He was ridiculous drinking a cup,
A cup of killing squirming booze,
A cup of mortal drastic hemlock,
    Wishing luck and happy days
    To everybody in Athens
    Ready for hell and hereafter,
    Ready for anything,
O I guess he was ridiculous, allright.

Why does nobody remember the name of the judge
who fixed him?
Why does nobody remember the name of the doctor
who shook the fatal booze?
Why does a rum-tum-tiddle world go on talking
Socrates and Socrates thousands and thousands
of years?

Stephen Crane

Before fame came to him he was scornful of it.
After fame arrived he was still scornful of it.
He asked himself how shall men of facts deal with poems,
    and how shall men of poems deal with facts?
In London his woman filled fourteen cob pipes
    with tobacco and stood them in a row on his
    writing table each morning.
The day's work was done and it was time to quit
    when the last pipe was smoked.
He died far on a blue star hunting the answer
    why steel is steel and mist is mist.

Who Was Hannah Adams?

She was the first woman in America to earn a living by
writing books.
She lost her mother when she was two years old.
She saw her father bankrupt when she was seventeen.
She learned Latin, Greek, Hebrew, Logic, and
        Geography
from ministry students boarding in her father's house.
While the armies of George Washington marched back and
        forth and up and down eight long smoky smoky years
She was teaching school and making lace.
She wrote books on religion,
        histories of the Jews and of New England.
She read so many books in order to write her own,
        that she nearly lost her eyes.
She never married,
She drank much tea,
        and her snuff box was always by her.
She died in Massachusetts in 1832, seventy-seven years old,
        the first woman to have a grave in the
                Mount Auburn Cemetery.
It would not look wrong if
        on her grave they had placed
                a teapot
                a snuff box and a
                little row of books.

[Tom Edison]

Tom Edison works like hell and sleeps four hours a day.
Tom Edison putters around with messages to the stars,
How to harness new fire hiding somewhere,
How to pry open new mouths of song
    loosening tongue-tied stones.
The choice is baggy pants, easy shoes to stand in,
    and a corner with noises cut off.
So Tom Edison works like hell and sleeps four hours a day.

John James Audubon

He lay on his back three weeks every day all day long under
  a tree where two birds were building a nest.

He wanted to learn, from the testimony of his own eyes,
  how birds build nests, from the first sticks and straws to
  the last.

He painted a thousand birds, in colors, life size, making
  memoranda of the length of bill, wing, claw, eye.

He carried in his stride and eyes long impressions of wings,
  tall trees, crotches of oaks and beeches, and singing
  neighbors of warm rain and blue sky.

Stephen Pearl Andrews

This lawyer in Houston, Texas, was driven from the city with his wife and baby one night in 1843.

He should have spoken few words or none with reference to African slavery and the equality of white and black races before the law; the mob called him names not worthy to print.

However, he went to England and tried to negotiate a loan from Great Britain to Texas for the purchase of slaves.

In Boston, then, he opened a school for the teaching of the new art of shorthand writing, moving on to New York to carry on publications advocating reform in spelling.

He learned Hebrew, Sanscrit, Chinese, but these were only three of the thirty-two languages he could read.

How natural he should then formulate a new language, Alwato, a universal tongue to be learned the world over and make Mankind as one!

How natural he should write *The Basic Outline of Universology*, a beautiful, earnest, crazy book, showing how all men would be brothers and all women sisters, if they should all learn the world over to speak Alwato.

Why should there not be epitaphs to beloved people who fail?

Iron Jaw

The Pilgrim father clutches a law book under his arm
Fingers of a hand close round the covers and pages.
And his jaws are shut irrevocably with iron resolve.
Drink and the devil, gamblers, whores and thieves,
The law book says they shall die.
Irrevocably, from iron resolves, they shall die.
It is the written voice of God they shall die.

Protest Poems

"Billy Sunday," the first poem in this section, is a rough first draft of the well-known poem, printed here for the first time. He had already published a version in two radical journals, *The Masses* and the *International Socialist Review*, but Sandburg's editor at Henry Holt asked for major changes, and the poet revised his strong indictment of Billy Sunday.

Philip Yannella, in *The Other Carl Sandburg*, wrote that the originality of "To a Contemporary Bunkshooter" (the title of the poem as it appeared in its revised version) "lay in its hard-boiled tone and its insulting language . . . :[it] was a poison-pen letter, an up-against-the-wall, ripsnorting denunciation that echoed all the traditions of literary and oratorical cursing." The first draft is even more pointed and pungent, in both language and subject. Sandburg says specifically that Sunday and William Randolph Hearst were in cahoots: "Hearst is boosting your game—you certainly always did belong with the whores."

"Both Ways" indicts two-faced politicians in the radical tradition. "[Finger Pointer]" puts forth an "I" who can point out the scoundrels of public life so that the people can know what the "I" knows. This was the position of the radical, investigative reporter of the Progressive Era: expose those who misuse the public trust and the "roof falls" on the evildoers. Sandburg obviously believed in this radical romantic dream when he worked on *The Day Book* until it folded in 1917. World War I and the Red Scare that followed were largely responsible for Sandburg's turning to a safer journalism—movie reviewer and columnist.

"[Wreck a Bank]" obviously belongs to the early period of Sandburg's life in Chicago. The safecracker, when caught, was sent to prison for twenty years; the white-collar banker who bled funds from a bank and wrecked it paid for good lawyers and was not punished.

"[Portrait of a Lady]" is an early draft of "Magical Confusion," a poem about Mrs. Potter Palmer. Sandburg loathed Mrs. Palmer, doyen of Chicago society, fully as much as he detested Billy Sunday. "[Portrait of a Lady]," recently added to the Sandburg Collection at the University of Illinois Library, like the first draft of "Billy Sunday," is raw and crude and forceful. Sandburg's revisions for "Magical Confusion" made the poem more acceptable for possible publication—though he did not publish it—but also diminished its power.

"A Talk with God" can be seen as the development of ideas in the "Billy Sunday" poems. Sandburg charged that the Reverend Sunday, in cahoots with businessmen, urged workers to accept their lot in exchange for promised rewards in heaven. The worker in "A Talk with God" rejects Sunday's notion and even rejects the existence of a divinity—unless God gives him a job in which he will not be laid off. With such a job in hand, the worker says, "I will believe/You are god."

In "Quotes" Sandburg contrasts Collis P. Huntington, the railroad robber baron, and Albert R. Parsons, one of the Haymarket defendants. Sandburg charged that Huntington made his fortune through bribery while Parsons knew that workers were ignorant "because they are poor, and poor because they are robbed."

"Quotes" appears to be an early poem, but "On Account of This Is a Free Country" was more likely written during the late 1940s. In an early draft of the poem, H. V. Kaltenborn, not Mr. Wafflehorn, is the name of the conservative radio commentator. In changing "Kaltenborn" to

"Wafflehorn" Sandburg moves from the particular to the general. The subject of the poem, of course, is that of control of the news by advertisers. The influence of advertisers on the content of newscasts remains a live issue fifty years after the poem was first written.

Billy Sunday

You come along tearing your shirt and talking about Jesus.
I want to know what the hell you know about Jesus.
Jesus had a way of talking soft and everybody except a few
    bankers and higher-ups among the con men liked to
    have this Jesus around because he was soothing and
    helped the sick and gave people hope.
You come along with a diarrhea of words, shaking your fist
    and calling all of us damn fools, froth of your own spit
    slobbering over your lips, blabbing and blabbing we're
    all going to hell and you know all about it.

I've read Jesus' words. I know what he said.
He never came near real decent people but they felt easier
    when he passed. It was your crowd of bankers and
    businessmen that hired the sluggers and murderers that
    put Jesus out of the game.
I say it was the same bunch that's backing you that nailed
    the nails into the hands of this Jesus of Nazareth. I
    know just as much about this Jesus of Nazareth as you
    do and I know he had lined up against him the same
    crooks and strong-arm men that are lined up with you
    paying your way.

This Jesus guy threw out something fresh and beautiful from
    his person wherever he passed along. The smell of his
    body, touch of his hands, catch in his voice made
    women and children feel safe and happy about God.
But you, Billy Sunday—you're only the dirty smokestack of
    a glue factory and you put a smut on every human
    blossom that listens to the raucous yawp of your
    bawling gibberish.

I like a man that's got guts and can pull off a great original
performance, but you, Billy Sunday—hell, you're only a
cheap salesman, a real American bunk artist selling and
selling for hard American dollars a cheap imitation of
the stuff this Jesus guy said ought to be free as air and
sunlight. I tell you you're an imitation and they're all
getting your number.
And now Hearst has picked you up—along with the
railroads and the banks and all the other big-business
crooks, Hearst is boosting your game—you certainly
always did belong with the whores.
If it would do any good I would vote for a law saying that
mutts running loose like you ought to have their
testicles cut out—but it wouldn't do any good so long
as you've got your leather tongue and your leather
lungs and your leather conscience.

Men you have called lousy are not half as lousy as you are.
Men you have called syphilitic and rotten are not half as
syphilitic and rotten as you are.
Sometimes I wonder what sort of pups born from mongrel
bitches there are in the world less heroic, less typic of
historic greatness than you.

You tell poor people living in shanties that Jesus is going to
fix it up all right with them by giving them mansions in
the skies after they're dead and the worms have eaten
'em.
You tell poor people they don't need more money on
payday and even if it is fierce to be out of a job, Jesus'll
fix that all right—all they got to do is take Jesus the way
you say.
I'm telling you this Jesus guy wouldn't stand for the stuff
you're handing out. The reason the bankers and
corporation lawyers of Jerusalem sent their sluggers

and murderers after Jesus was because he wouldn't play
their game.

Why don't you go away somewhere and sit by yourself a
whole day in a toilet,
On a stool all by yourself, sitting there with your chin in
your hands,
Think it all over, empty your bowels to a finish, and ask
yourself if you ain't about as coarse and crooked a
grafter as any of 'em in the penitentiaries of the United
States or the pits of hell you tell us about.

I've been out to this suburb of Jerusalem they called
Golgotha, where they nailed him, and I know if the
story is straight it was real blood ran from his hands
and the nail-holes and it was real blood spurted out
where the spear of the Roman soldier was rammed in
between the ribs of this Jesus you talk about.
I won't take any bunk from you or anybody else about it—
you gotta show me where you're pouring out the blood
of your life instead of grabbing piles of American silver
dollars and keeping the mints working overtime.

I want blood instead of bunk in my religion.

Both Ways

I carry a thousand faces.
A ragbag rigadoon hugger-mugger of faces.
I shake hands with a Roman Catholic and let him know
    that I wish well for the Mother of Jesus and I know the
    Magnificat and the sign of the cross and the uses of
    holy water.
I shake hands with a Guardian of Liberty and I let him
    know I think there's a little bull-con about the Mother
    of Jesus being a Holy Virgin.
         I play 'em both ways.
I am running for governor of a great corn state in the
    Mississippi Valley.

[1913]

[Finger Pointer]

I am the finger pointer.
I am the shadow lurking unseen back of the lawyers, the
     jury, and the judge.
I am the only one who sees the jury-fixers and the money-
     passers, and I know when a go-between has reached
     the judge.
I hear when a political backer telephones the judge at his
     home or in a club room whispers a talismatic word into
     the judge's ear so that all words from the bench when
     the case comes to trial are written beforehand the same
     as the lines in a play for mimics who lick their lips,
     wrinkle their brows, and take on the look of
     deliberation.
I point my finger and they only, the maskers and fakers
     only, know what I mean and I, tracking them in offices
     and streets and to their bedsides when they take off
     their clothes for sleep—I am the only one they are
     afraid of—I am the only one that makes life a blurred
     chart or a mad wreck to them.
When the people know what I know, then the finger
     pointer changes from a shadow into a real shape with a
     tongue and newspapers and police and mobs behind it,
     then the roof falls in and walls crash and old, holy
     things are broken.

[Wreck a Bank]

Be a peteman* and wreck a bank from the outside
    and you get twenty years.
Be a banker and wreck a bank from the inside
    and you get what you get.
There are different kinds of bank wreckers,
       those who take a chance, outside the law,
       and those who know the law and take no chances.

*Safecracker—ED.

[Portrait of a Lady]

The body of the lady,
Carried feet first (or head first)—
For the lady had feet and head
Similarly formed
Like a Slav woman
With a handkerchief of knickknacks—
The body was carried in a box to a railroad train
And taken north to her winter home.

The thoughts of the undertaker
Crept into none of the newspapers.
The comment of the embalmers was not quoted.
Whether one handling the preservative fluids
The oil that fights for a few days the attacks
Of the swarming eaters and creepers,
Whether one said, "You shoot it into this old squirt
Just like anybody else."
Whether this was an occurrence of fact
There is no record.

Cameramen taking stills and movie film
Hovered as a flotilla of truth hunters
At the funeral.
        The last magical confusion
Of crossed spotlights of rainbow color
Wherewith the lady invested her years and days
Came like a diminuendo flutter of violins
In the newspaper stories of the funeral—
The annals bore witness to the cortege,
The appointments and pronouncements,
The distinguished character, the impressive beauty
Of a lady's funeral.

The mausoleum itself
Gained mention as "the most beautiful in Graceland
    Cemetery."
And the shovel whereupon blew the words, "Dust to dust,
Ashes to ashes," lay the next day speaking of Æsop's fables
To an angleworm that writhed a slithy tove
In a sun-warm layer of sod.

The maker of allegories to be read by proud people
Might tell how the little bugs held a conclave
With a chuckling spokesman, "We got her all right, all
    right."

And a painter of pictures
Looking for the magical confusion
Of crossed spotlights of rainbow color
Might try his brush on a Slav woman
With a heart hammering great wishes against her ribs,
A baby sitting in the hood of her left arm,
A handkerchief of knickknacks in her right hand.

A Talk with God

My job is a little thing
And a boss whose head is
Full of funny thoughts
Changing like the wind
And quick as the weather,
    The boss,
He can take my job away
And throw me on the street
To slouch with the hungry men
Whenever he takes it
Into his damn head to fire me.

For myself I don't care,
I can bum and scrape along
But the kids and woman home,
    They can't bum.
Hell breaks loose for them
They worry and cry and go
Without things they want
When the boss takes it
Into his head to fire me.

    For myself
I don't care a goddam
But sometimes I say,
"O God, if you are a God,
    Come on
And show you are a God.
    Make good,
Get me a job nobody
Can take away from me:
Then I will believe
    You are God."

Quotes

Collis P. Huntington, thick and big-boned, upstanding, with an eye for the Union Pacific and its Golden Spike, he was telling no names when he said:
"If you have to pay money to have the right thing done, it is only just and fair to do it."
There were those then as now who knew exactly what he was talking about and why he was naming no names and no specific sums from giver, which was himself, to the taker who heard him say it was just and right.

If they hadn't hanged Mr. Albert R. Parsons in Chicago in 1888—by the neck till he was dead—it might be less remembered that he said: "The working classes are ignorant because they are poor, and poor because they are robbed."

On Account of This Is a Free Country

We don't have to listen to Mister Wafflehorn.
We tune him in and get a scuttle of what he's got
Or tune him out and give him the gate, the air,
The wide and circumambient air
By authority of the federal communications commission.
    We tune him in and let him go with his
"Good evening, everybody," which we know includes
Those of us who happen to be tuned in and leaves out
Everybody of the other millions listening elsewhere
To other commentators, other programs on the dial—
    Or with due respect and by an eighth-inch twist
of a deliberate thumb, we dial him out, shut him off
    On account of this is a free country.

    What we like best is where Hank winds up:
        "Good-night—and here
        is Kyle Rance
        for the Deep Oil Company."
This gives the idea, like an alibi, like a whitewash,
Like a supersuds rinso dreft duz ivory flakes cleansing,
Like Mister Wafflehorn ain't been speaking a breath
In behalf and to the behoof of The Deep Oil Company
And what's commercial we get from Kyle Rance
And nothing commercial indeed indeed from Hank
    Wafflehorn.

Now the way some of us take it is like this
And a few other listening galoots string along:
    Joe Pool of Pennsylvania belongs in the picture,
    Him being the big-shot say-so of Deep Oil and
    What gives in Deep Oil goes back to Joe Pool.
Mister Pool has views, opinions, slants at the news

And Mister Wafflehorn, being a scholar and a gentleman,
Has his independent views, opinions, slants at the news.
  So far, so good,
  And we know Wafflehorn agrees, concurs.

From there on it ain't so nice, may be bad manners
To let on Joe Pool tells Wafflehorn what to say.
Joe Pool wouldn't do that and any time he should try
We would find Wafflehorn is nobody's Charlie McCarthy.*
So seem the facts, no depositions or affidavits needed.

From there on we can try to take the fool thing apart
And spot the bugs and eliminate the bugs one by one—
We can try but it's liable to be a laugh—horsefeathers—
Like the man who stood out in the rain to catch
A water supply with his outstretched arms holding a sieve.

We can imagine we're dumb as Archie of Duffy's Tavern.
Or we can see ourselves sitting bright among the Quiz Kids†
Never answering the dumb questions never asked us—like—
Does Mister Wafflehorn, the dean of radio commentators,
Have any slight inkling from day to day, week to week,
Of what Joe Pool thinks, says, does, wants, wishes?
Would Wafflehorn under any conditions whatsoever
slant the news, preach and teach, cry out loud
Any propositions that would bother Joe Pool and irk him?

Now these many years Deep Oil and Pool sponsor Hank,
Meaning Hank the Wafflehorn, Hank the commentator
    dean.
Can it be that Hank pleases Deep Oil. Hank pleases Pool?
We don't know—we deduce, infer, presume—we don't
    know.

---

*Edgar Bergen's dummy in the popular radio program.—ED.
†"Duffy's Tavern" and "Quiz Kids" were popular radio programs.—ED.

This we do know—Pool is right of center—so is Hank.
Should Pool go center or left would Hank go likewise?
We don't know—we merely know they both now hate the
    left,
The vermin, the varmints, the vicious and viscous left,
conceived in sin, hell-born, hell-bound, the left, the left.
slimy, inhuman, subhuman, out of cesspools, the left, the
    left.

Should Hank go left and Pool stay right of center—then
    what?
We don't know a thing, baby—only the event itself could
    tell.
Pool might say, "Throw Wafflehorn out on his tin ear,"
And then again Pool might say, "Let him have his head."

Where Pool is he could say it either way—*it's his show.*
Where Hank is he would take whatever was handed him.
And if he didn't have a script he would ad lib.
He knows what he wants to say for himself on his own
Without anybody else cutting in, either Deep Oil or Pool.
    So we tune him in and get a scuttle of suds
Or tune him out and give him the gate, the air,
On account of this is a free country—
    "Good-night—and here
    is Kyle Rance
    for the Deep Oil Company."

116

Nature Poems

Sandburg and his wife liked to take long walks in all kinds of weather, sometimes in wild areas. Sandburg was often silent and brooding on these walks. He was a sharp observer of what he saw, and the techniques he learned from the Imagists served him well as he wrote about stars and fires, the bleak landscapes of February, the broken summers in October, and the frosts of November.

The Last Star

Daylight crawls the street.
Night creeps away.
Farewells come from tired stars
Keeping the last night watch.
Turned ashes one by one they leave,
The last of all the stars calling,
"The night is gone,
Good-by for tonight—and good-by."

In the spells of toil
Down the long day on the job,
I think of you:
The last morning star
Glimmering over the roofs.

Fires

Lingering fires of the West subside,
Embers of day now pass and flicker.
Sundown shadows fall on the lake
And a city of stars on placid water
Mirrors and gleams and silently hovers.

February

Leafless, stark, immemorial,
The trees have gazed down on the desolate grass.

Under the snow the hills have slept
And the heart of the long-gone summer.

Deep and far
In the core of the hollows and uplands,
Waits, only waits, like sky and sod,
The silent and beautiful girl-child, Spring.

October

Out of the broken summer
The lone red leaf is a crushed memory
Dying while the wind and rain
Mourn the death babble of the summer.
The rain drums play a dead march daylong
And nightlong the wind cries in a treetop
The heart's regret of parting
And the ruin of the roses.

November Nocturne

The night-mist hovers on the hills.
The slow creek winds between the slopes,
Friend of the stones and soil and moss
With its persistent, glad-idling little notes.

The high moon trails its stuff on the sky.
In dim-blue backgrounds stars of silver follow,
Redoubled in hoof-shaped pools by the waterside.

Cattle stand motionless, calm.
A lone tall tree looks down
Where a gash on a hillside looms
Scarfed in mystical vapor.

The grasses stiffen and shine
With hoar-frost: on the weeds white ashes
Glisten. We loiter and wait. Lower veers
The handle of the Dipper. An owl hoots.
A breeze stirs. The creek babbles on. We muse
Amid the great eternal heartbeats of
The Near-at-hand, the Infinite.

Literary and Movie Criticism

Sandburg was not a professional critic; he seldom reviewed books in the popular journals of his time, but he was widely read and had strong artistic opinions about literature, music, photography, and painting. In conversation he willingly talked at length about other poets. In "[He Sez / I Sez]" he held up to scorn the popular poetry of late Victorianism with its romantic portrait of home, country, dogs, the honest poor, and patriotism. He asserted with some irony that, according to one literary theory, a poem had to have meaning or it wasn't a poem, that a poem must not have mystery in it. Sandburg the pro-worker radical clearly wanted to write poems that the people could understand, but one must not then assume that Sandburg thought the people could not understand difficult poetry. Sandburg believed in the ability of a mass audience to go beyond conventional verse, to understand more than the literary intellectuals might expect, including poems of mystery.

In "Good and Bad Poets" he returns to the subject of bad poets who write romantically about home, children, and apple pie. This 1913 poem saucily calls for the eradication of the bad poets in his midst.

When he was a student at Lombard College, Sandburg read and admired the works of William James, but he never quite "cottoned" to Henry James. He had problems with Henry James's abandoning the United States, and he especially disliked the coterie of James scholars. Sandburg's class bias shows in the poem about Henry James, of course, but he is sensible in his questioning of the Henry James scholarly industry.

From 1920 to 1927 Sandburg was film critic for the *Chicago Daily News*. His "Successful Films" expresses his views on the inanity of most historical films produced in Hollywood at the time. What Sandburg wanted in the presentation of Jesus or Shakespeare was a picture of life in their times: Jesus and the fishermen repairing their nets and talking about fishing conditions, Shakespeare in a tavern listening to the groundlings and barkeep talking about love.

[He Sez / I Sez]

And he sez to me, "A poem ought to have a meaning."
And I sez, "Yes, of course, it ought to should."
And he sez, "I mean, there ought to be a meaning to a poem
    so everybody understands it."
And I sez, "Sure, of course, why, if a poem ain't clear, plain
    as the nose on a man's face, plain as a fish, a mackerel,
    a salt herring, plain as a piece of cheese, why, it ain't a
    poem."

Yes, a book of verse should have answers in the back of the
    book, the same as an arithmetic.
Poems should tell about mother, home and heaven, about
    our flag and our country, about sweet children who
    have left hearts aching, about cripples and dogs and
    sweet magnolias, especially about flowers and about
    honest hearts that beat beneath ragged coats, and about
    anything except superincumbent cucumbers.

Mystery we leave to the fortune-tellers; we mustn't put
    mystery in poetry.

Good and Bad Poets

Will you tell us how many poets in America should in
    justice be put to death?
Will you tell us how to get laws for the public hanging or
    electrocution of bad poets?
Will you tell us how to pick out bad poets for hanging or
    electrocution as farmers throw out apples for the cider
    mill?
Have you seen apples sunrise red on the outside all mushy
    brown to the core inside?

[1913]

[Henry James]

Henry James was a poor fish.
I'm tired of hearing about Henry James.
I repeat it, he was a poor fish
    and didn't know the way to the post office.
You can have him, bruddah bones.
I've read him, I know his drift.
I get him coming and going.
I can use him, some good spots
    and quite a lot of rot
    and the rot doesn't stink
    it exudes an odor
    it delivers an effluvia
    if you know what I mean.

Thirty-five years ago
    there was Ez Pound
    writing endless praise
    of the endless Henry James—
so Pound up and quits the U.S.A.
    leaving us behind
    precisely like H.J.
    hooting at the ways of the U.S.A.
    and what we're doing
    sure looks like a foozle.

So H.J. becomes a British subject
Pound makes Fascist broadcasts
and that is the way each wanted it
    while they were doing it.
        And it must be okay
        for they studied about it
        and they wrote about it
they put it all down in black and white.

Why did Owen Wister put it in his book,
his hearing Oliver Wendell Holmes Jr. say,
"The books of Henry James might as well have
　　　been written on white paper with white ink."
Or again, as to H.J., "Fifty years of polite
　　　conversation and nothing doing."???

Why did Matthiessen write on and on
　　　pages and pages about H.J.
　　　a whole book about Henry James
And then make a fadeout　a sliding away
　　　by his own hand　almost as though saying,
"I put out my hand to Henry James but he wasn't
　　　there　goom-bye now　goom-bye."

Henry had a brother, William.
I have my money on William.
There was a writer and a mind.
He bet on the U.S.A. and the Family of Man.
He was sorry for his brother Henry.

　　　He wrote to Henry, something like,
"You're getting in too deep, you're getting
　　　tangled and strangled in your own made
　　　abstrusities and obscurantisms—watch
　　　your step, brother!"
And he heard from Henry, something like,
　　　"I'm neither British nor American—maybe
　　　I should have stayed in the U.S.A.
　　　where I had roots."

I repeat, H.J. was a poor fish.
I'm tired of hearing about him.
I'd rather hear more about his brother
　　　who could find his way to the post office

who knew a hawk from a handsaw
who was a Friend of Man
and not afraid of People.

Why these books, one and another,
more and more books about Henry James.
There he is on his shelf.
You can go and read him any time.
He is what he is and you can take him
        or leave him.
He's an aristocrat who could never begin
        to understand Franklin, Jefferson,
        Lincoln, Tom Ferril of Colorado, Ole
        Rolvaag of South Dakota, H. L. Davis of
        Most Any Old Place in the New World.
He's a snob if by snob we mean a man born and
        raised in Boston who hungers and thirsts by
        Jesus he must yet somehow become a British subject.

        You can have him, gents.
        Pile up your books about him, about H.J.
Why should I be meeting pathetic screwballs who spend
        so much time reading about how to read Henry James
        they don't have time to read the Master Himself?

        As I said, gents, you can have him, I'll take his brother.
        I'll take Robert Frost, Archie MacLeish, Walt Whitman,
        Edwin Ford Piper, John Steinbeck, Willa Cather, Frank
        Dobie, Stevie Benet, and forty others I could name.

What I would like to say, with all due respect, gents,
        I'm about fed up with the Henry James clique.
        There has been just about enough
                of this pap sucking and foot kissing.

It wouldn't have come easy on H.J.
   to have lived on to where
   he could read Mr. Maugham saying
Henry James with all his anxious trying
never could get the hang of how the English speak
and his English characters didn't have
   the speech of the English.
It would have hurt H.J. to hear that from such an
   Englishman as Maugham.
      Maugham was sorry for Henry James
      and I am likewise.
    I believe Maugham knows his onions.

I remember when Ben Stolberg made a point.
He had seen fellows on the way to the office
   reading the Hearst papers
   and managing on entry to the office
   to be holding the New York Times
   showing they were hep
   to what was going on in the world.
Likewise there are the ambulant somnambulists
   who expect to be rated very literary
   something more than mere culture vultures
   by riding on the coattails of Henry James
   by prattling of the adumbrations
   and the mauve mists of H.J.—
      naive hunks of cheese
      hoping to be rated hypersensitive
      and exquisite of registration.

Successful Films

All the old pictures of Jesus Christ and William Shakespeare
   Go strong on whiskers and goatees.
They are not as movies of men talking and walking in old
   Jerusalem or Stratford-on-Avon.

   Why should any one bring me,
   (An asker of questions)
   The imaginings of ancient artists,
Showing only the whims of barbers and a distinction of
   haircuts and shaves
Between the Man of Nazareth and the English play writer?

   How the people
   Would line the sidewalks
   To see a movie
From the shore of Galilee with Jesus sitting around an old
   shanty
With a bunch of fishermen fixing their nets, talking about
   how the wind blew last week or last year

   or a reel
Of Shakespeare at a stein of ale in an old tavern
   Sitting with his dark eyes in a corner
Listening to the talk of stone masons and shoemakers
Telling the bartender how they love their wives
   or women they knew before they met their wives.

African-Americans

In both "[A Goner]" and "[Love or Cheap Love]" Sandburg uses the word "nigger," a word that today is jarring to readers. We know from his other poems and his prose pieces about the Chicago Race Riots of 1919 that Sandburg was sympathetic to African-Americans. He was revolted by lynching, understood the simple words of a grieving mother, detested the lynchers who "leer and sneer." In this case, Sandburg is accurately recording the language of redneck lynchers and of a terrible time in our history.

"[Love or Cheap Love]" is a meditation on the "cheap love" of white men for African-American women. Again, Sandburg uses language as it would have been used in the context of the poem, though he was repulsed by it. It is well documented that white planters and overseers freely took sexual advantage of slave women, and the sexual exploitation of African-American women has continued throughout the twentieth century. On the streets of Chicago, in cities in the South, and across the country as Sandburg made his reading tours, he saw the results of these "love" stories. How would these "love" stories end? Would cheap love result in cheap children? Were some of these love stories less than cheap? In this poem Sandburg plays to human mystery and to the tragedy of the octoroon in America.

"John Arthur Johnson" is another poem now difficult to read. In "[Love and Cheap Love]" Sandburg clearly believed that most of the "affairs" between white men and black women were "cheap love." In this poem he deals with a famous black boxer who used white prostitutes. In other poems Sandburg had suggested that women turned to prostitution because of economic and social conditions, and he was generally sympathetic to their plight. In "John Arthur Johnson" the "I" of the poem seems puzzled, wanting to know why sex should not be for love. He ponders why a white prostitute sells herself "for the money of any white man or the money of any black man," but the "I" is clearly uneasy envisioning a white woman with a black man. Sandburg does not condemn, but in his questioning he reveals that old racial stereotypes die hard.

[A Goner]

Head, legs, torso, the nigger is a goner.
The stump eaten by a street bonfire.
The faces, forty faces, leer and sneer in a circle
Around the night's work, another nigger gone.

The body here was a creature.
His mother called him a man and said, "God made him,
I brought him in the world for God."
These faces circling around the burnt stumps, the cinder
     head,
These faces say, "This nigger was a son of a bitch."

[Love or Cheap Love]

White man, you have loved many nigger women?
These faces that pass, your face is in their eyes and skin.
Your blood is in their blood, your passion poured out here.
White man, you have laid hot kisses on nigger women,
You have taken time and wild hours here.
It is all over these faces that pass.
The last chapter of this love story is yet to come.
It is easy to love and forget when love is cheap.
Yet tomorrow never is willing to call itself yesterday.
Tomorrow stands on its own legs and tells its own story,
Makes itself a witness on love or cheap love.

John Arthur Johnson

He won a world's championship as a fistfighter and for a
   black man it was an honor past any other he might
   bring home to the old mammy whose milk he grew on.
And then he bought a saloon with tall looking glasses and
   sixty-dollar brass cuspidors—and after that he went out
   and bought white girls, white women, to be had for the
   buying.
Now you may hunt all day in the rubbish of these facts and
   get nowhere and find nothing that gives you the kick
   you get after a good highball, a Robert Chambers story,
   or a front-page New York World scandal.
All I want from you is an explanation why a slim white girl
   with red lips and dark eyes impressionistic as peaches,
   roses, night stars or sea mist,
Sells her white shoulders, sells her white legs, sells her
   white belly, for the money of any white man or the
   money of any black man,
Or for anything else than kisses from lips worth
   remembering till the dead wagon comes—for anything
   else than love, memories, and dreams.

143

World War I

Like most American Socialists, Sandburg opposed World War I, but when the United States entered the war he broke with the party and supported Woodrow Wilson. The poems in this section, from 1915–1917, indicate Sandburg's moods and observations about that brutal war.

Sandburg's anti-war poems appeared in his *Complete Poems*, and we published others in *Billy Sunday and Other Poems*. "May, 1915" contrasts the violence in Europe, meaningless jabber in Washington, D.C., and New York, and the beauty of spring blossoms in Illinois. Politics, commerce, violent destruction, and blossoms are all intermingled in a slice of life from that world.

By 1917, however, the poet writes that lilacs are sparse that spring. Logically the reason was simple: not enough rain. But are Americans, now involved in the war, right to see the sparse blooms in terms of the terrible conflict in which they now have a part? By that winter of 1917 American troops with others from many countries are crawling in the snow, ready to kill others crawling in the snow. The king (is it the czar? the kaiser?) thinks he controls the land, but the people at this point believe that the king (the czar, the kaiser) is dreaming. By 1917 Sandburg had decided to support the American war effort, and he believed the old order in Europe was about to change dramatically.

"Everybody in Town Has Been Drillin' and Drillin' for the Big Parade" was written at the time of the June 1916 Preparedness Day parade in Chicago, and appeared in *The Day Book*. It has a hypnotic, rhythmical effect in describing how, months before America's declaration of war, the public is preparing for the impending hostilities.

Although Sandburg at this time was still anti-war, his stance in the poem is to report the activities and to write of the consensus views of Chicago citizens: "we ought to be in some kind of shape to fight IF we have to fight."

"The Woman on the Billboards" is set in Chicago after war had been declared in 1917; it appeared in *The Day Book* on May 16. The newspaper had been carrying stories for some time about the anti-union Harry Moir, owner of the Hotel Morrison, and also stories about illegal activities in the hotel. Sandburg had written Alfred Harcourt on February 4, 1916, that Billy Sunday was said to own stock in that hotel, which was "persistently notorious in Chicago courts for the studied and civilized vice, the commercialized night pleasure which is so much harder to look at than natural depravity."

The Day Book described one of the Hotel Morrison billboards: "A poster of eighteen chorus girls smiling over bare, pink shoulders. . . ." Robert Reid has properly pointed out the contrasting images in the poem: "The promise of gaiety in Chicago's night clubs is set against the sobering reality of American fighting men lying wounded in European trenches." Sandburg's class consciousness is clear throughout the poem. Moir's night club is for the wealthy with their "boiled shirts." Moir was anti-union and profiting on prostitution, but even Marshall Field III and Joseph Medill Patterson, scions of Chicago's most prominent families, joined sons of Poles and Bohunks in the American army. War profiteering at the Morrison and death on the battlefields of France are powerfully contrasting images.

May, 1915

Amid the jabber of taxes, politics, and telegraph stories
    from Washington, D.C., and New York, N.Y.,
And amid the war cries of the Germans smashing at Verdun
    and the French countering while the Irish rebels die in
    the streets of Dublin and Russian contingents land at
    Marseilles,
And amid the hike of infantry, push of cavalry, and whirr of
    aeroplanes on the Mexican border, the presidential
    booms unlimbering axles of their bandwagons,
Two cherry trees in an Illinois backyard put out one by one
    hundreds of blossoms, jonquils broke yellow, and tulips
    broke red, and stood in the sun.

[1915]

[Lilacs of 1917]

Sparse lilacs of 1917:
The rain roots are wrong this year.
I understand.
Many others are puzzled.
It is a smile that trembles.
It comes and goes.
It is there and it isn't.
Lilacs this year: I understand.

Christmas Cartoon, 1917

A window frames a picture:
Ten men crawl on snow,
Under the wind,
Under the needles and knives of wind
Piling the snow in changing curves,
Ten men on their bellies
Ten red zigzags,
Under the shoveling winds.

The man at the window eats bread with cow's butter
and mutters a throaty guttural:
I am the king of the land and it is all mine.

Between mouthfuls in the late dawn, in the shiver of
needles and knives outside, he speaks to his heart,
he dozes in a dream:
I am the king of the land and it is all mine.

Everybody in Town Has Been Drillin' and Drillin' for the Big Parade

Chicago has been turned into a big training camp this week.

They're drillin' and drillin'.

From the top roofs of State Street stores out to the streets and back alleys of the stockyards district they are drillin' and drillin'.

Nearly every shop, factory, and store of any size in Chicago has been at it now—drillin' and drillin'.

Men and women—boys and girls—mothers and fathers—kids and kiddos—drillin' and drillin'.

It swept the town.

"Hep—hep—hep—dress to the right—dress to the left—column right."

Bosses and straw bosses and day workers—fellows at the top and bottom of the payroll—marching along in platoons—drillin' and drillin'.

And now on Preparedness Day all these marchers and drillers from all over Chicago are melted together into one big parade, the longest procession of marchers that ever hit the streets of Chicago.

Hours and hours of marchers, blocks and blocks, miles and miles of hikers.

"Hep—hep—hep—hayfoot, strawfoot, bellyful o' bean soup—right, left"—and so they go on—young and old, fat and lean, Americans all.

A son of a Civil War veteran sings
"There was an old soldier and he
      had a wooden leg,
He had no tobacco, no tobacco
      could he beg.

Another old soldier and he had a
    wooden box
And he always had tobacco in
    his old tobacco box."

Flags—and the downtown district is all flags—a forest
of flags.

And under these rows and festoons of flags the
marchers go—hour on hour—miles of marchers.

And what's the idea? Well, something like this:

Let all other nations keep their hands off the United
States. We're going to settle our own hash, work out our
own destiny, and we ought to be in some kind of shape to
fight IF we have to fight.

[1916]

The Woman on the Billboards

I like dancing, Bill—and I like singing women—and I like fried chicken and the tickling ragtime of fiddles and horns, drums and saxophones.

And yet—this morning when I got off a streetcar after reading the news from places in the north of France, dark red places,

I saw Harry Moir's new poster on a billboard—a woman in a skirt to her knees—a woman balanced on her left leg—with her right leg pointed northwest—dancing on skates for a lot of gazooks in clawhammer coats and boiled shirts in the Hotel Morrison—

And I said to myself: I guess Harry Moir knows what he's doing, and maybe it's good for business, and maybe we ought to fight the war this way and have plenty of leg shows in all the hotels.

And I had a flash of some Chicago boy—maybe Marshall Field or Joe Patterson—maybe some Polak or Bohunk from back of the yards—

I have a flash of some Chicago boy with a red smash on the side of his head in a ditch in northern France calling: "For Christ's sake, pal, gimme some water."

[1917]

Ruminations

Sitting at his desk in his office or in his workroom at home, Sandburg reflected on his life, his world. He was sometimes happy, sometimes sad, but always questioning, probing, seeking answers, sometimes finding mysteries.

One of the most complex of these musing poems is "Acknowledgments," in which Sandburg draws on Sunday School teachings from his childhood, when he read the Bible in Swedish and in English, and on his knowledge of modern events. He is Whitmanesque in his encompassing of such diverse figures as Jesus, Shakespeare, Belshazzar, Nebuchadnezzar, Absolom, Harry Thaw, Philip Armour, and Marshall Field. Sandburg uses some of the most memorable biblical stories as he relates Nebuchadnezzar's madness, which leads him to eat grass, to Harry Thaw's madness, leading him to murder Stanford White. Sandburg makes connections between Jewish princes and royalty and the merchant princes of Chicago. In this poem he acknowledges the family of man, with its best and its worst. It is his variation on Whitman's "Chanting the Square Deific": adding evil to the godhead. In his poem Sandburg's man is both good and evil, just as both good and evil exist in biblical stories and in his contemporary society.

"Climbers" is a self-questioning poem. Sandburg notes that he began by writing descriptive, imagistic poems, then went on to write about the ironworkers on the highrise structures then a-building in Chicago. These "blasphemous" workers were the very stuff of poetry, and there is a plaintive note as Sandburg asks: "how many poems did I make" about these daredevil workers?

The two poems that follow, "Pigeons" and "Two Shapes in Gray," are remarkably different. In "Pigeons" the imagistic details of beauty and happiness are replaced by the solitary "I" alone "with silence and the gods of dust." The poems have a brooding quality, much emphasized in Sandburg's prose portrait of Lincoln, especially in *The War Years*. In "Two Shapes in Gray" the sparrows remind him of two men named Charles: Charles Lamb and Charles XII of Sweden. In Lamb's prose Sandburg found remarkable descriptions, and he was so intrigued by Charles XII that he considered writing a biography of the soldier-king.

"Two Girls and a Father," written about 1917, would appear to be a diary poem, the capturing of a moment in time. The chatter of the two little girls fills the house and pours out the window, while the drowsing father upstairs, continually awakened by his children, contemplates their fate. What will become of them? The poem is particularly poignant in biographical terms, for the Sandburgs' daughter Margaret developed epilepsy in 1921, and the second daughter, Janet, already slow to learn, suffered extensive brain damage after she was struck by an automobile in 1932. Sandburg could not know, when he wrote his poem, that these two daughters would be severely handicapped, would have to remain at home, and would never "go out in the world."

"Palooka and Champ" indicates how intimately Sandburg knew the Chicago world of gyms and prizefighting. In his journey through the city's netherworld, he must have come into contact with palookas with cauliflower ears and slurred speech, fighters who were going nowhere except toward public slaughter. He shared the great fear of all fighters, as of all poets, that success would be elusive.

"Green Hair," written in the winter of 1940, was part of what Sandburg called his experiment in "platform appearance." After interviewing the poet, Karl Detzer wrote that Sandburg thought of it as "a combination of the human voice reciting poetry with symphonic light effects and special music . . . that plays a major role. He sees this work performed against stage settings in shapes and colors that create moods, illusions, and play upon the emotions of listeners." Sandburg wrote three poems in this mode: "Mr. Baudelaire and His Green Hair," "Mr. Lincoln and His Gloves," and "Mr. Longfellow and His Boy."

"Mulligatawney" is truly a highly flavored mixture, with Sioux, Arabian, and American 1920s sayings. Pursuers of high culture are dealt with in his references to Wagner and the valkyries. Comic soup, with hot curries, is one recipe of love.

In "Mutt Born" Sandburg names his mixed-breed dog "McTeague," marking his admiration of the naturalist novelist Frank Norris. The qualities of the brutal, animalistic dentist in Norris's *McTeague* are not found, though, in Sandburg's comic creation of the dog without a pedigree.

The section ends with a poem to Walt Whitman, whose style and voice greatly influenced Sandburg. He pays his respects to the early Whitman, the daring poet of "Song of Myself," "Children of Adam," "Calamus," and "When Lilacs Last at the Dooryard Bloom'd," and rightly asks readers not to "forget him because he grew old and preached what once he sang." Sandburg's point is well taken, and applies to him as well. Sandburg's late poetry, after 1940 certainly, is often weak and derivative. We should not forget Sandburg; his mature poems are strong, and his best work will endure.

Acknowledgments

I make my acknowledgments to you,
Jesus, Shakespeare, Lincoln, *Mother Nature*
And to you Belshazzar, Nebuchadnezzar,
Absolom, Harry Thaw, Phil Armour, Marshall Field.
I say you dead are more real than people I see on the
    streetcars, in offices and restaurants, in parks and cigar-
    store hangouts.

Nine or ten great-grandmothers touching fingertips,
Span the time between the Illinois Man and the Man of
    Galilee.
And thirteen great-grandmothers or so cover the days
Between Belshazzar and Marshall Field, Absolom hanging
    by the hair and Harry Thaw in Matteawan.

Is the story honest-to-God? Nebuchadnezzar on his hands
    and knees fed on grass with milk cows of the
    Babylonian empire he ruled?
I only know he lived and died, sat in a chair while
    engineers, inventors, artists waited for the imperious
    say-so, the final yes or no of his lips.
I only know Phil Armour lived and died, sat in a chair
    while modern intercessors waited for the say-so, the
    prices and valuations, the yes or no of his mouth.
I only know Nebuchadnezzar and Phil Armour are both
    under the grassroots and their monuments are guesses
    on the weather tomorrow or next week.

Shakespeare? Lincoln?
The Stratford Man won the name of a nobody in his time.
The Springfield Man got a fool's bullet in his head and
    finished his life in the shadows of war.

From the tombs both of them laugh at nine-tenths of the
   books written about them.
From the tombs they ask why and why of schools,
   newspapers, and churches.
From the tombs they ask nothing, say nothing, expect
   nothing, keeping the silence of those who know.

To these beautiful dead ones—poets, kings, fools, killjoys
   and joymasters—to you I make my acknowledgments
   before I join you.

[1915]

Climbers

I began making poems of crags and eagles.
The molten red firestone—cool at last—
The high gray wings beating storm and azure:
    Why not poems of these?

And I began making poems of skyscrapers and structural
    iron workers.
Jimmy McNutt afoot on a girder veering mid-air . . . waving
    signals to an engineer down walls steeper than
    Chimborazo or the Matterhorn . . . catching red-molten
    rivets in a bucket . . . running a rat-tat-tat on corners
    and floors crazy as an eagle's crag in form and
    chaos . . .
Climbing day by day, floor by floor, till the roof at last spoke
    to the earth's arc . . .

Out of these red-necked blasphemous climbers—how many
    poems did I make?

Pigeons

They were all thieves,
Forty pigeons I saw flutter to the street
Picking the grain that lay on the stones.

One had purple wings and on her neck
The colors of the rainbow shining
When the feathers shifted in the sun.

All were happy,
Their wings drummed and thrummed
As they swung away without a single good-by on their
    fleering pinions,
Leaving me alone with silence and the gods of dust.

Two Shapes in Gray

On winter mornings when I eat breakfast I look out on a
   cherry tree where five gray sparrows sit and exchange
   gossip over the day's prospects.
And I have thought looking on gray wings in the snowy
   crotches of dark limbs against the morning west, I have
   thought often of two men named Charles.
One was a bookkeeper in a government office in London,
   stammered his words in the spoken tongue, took care
   of a beautiful sister who was out of her head, and
   between whiles wrote a book of stammering thoughts
   people love a hundred years after his funeral.
One was a Swedish soldier, routed a hundred thousand
   Russ with eight thousand Swedes in a night battle, and
   died young with a bullet between two ribs, becoming a
   precious memory of all young men who value the zest
   of personal danger.
The gray of these memories mingles with the gray of the five
   sparrows in a cherry tree winter mornings near my
   breakfast window.

Two Girls and a Father

The soprano of the six-year-old girl joins the contralto of
    her two-year-old sister.
They babble at each other a jargon of kid talk and it fills the
    house Sunday morning and runs out of the windows.
The father upstairs turns for a third consecutive nap and
    puts himself to sleep again with thoughts of what will
    become of his daughters when they grow up and go out
    in the world.

[circa 1917]

Palooka and Champ

The palooka is at the bottom.
Once he was a comer, an aspirant.
He represented X, the unknown.
He'll be a champ one of these
      pretty days: it was said.
Then he learned how to take it,
Hooks to the right and left,
Jabs to the jaw, the jugular, the heart,
Swings that landed heavy,
He took the haymaker, the kayo,
Rested his weary head on a cauliflower ear.
He couldn't hear the referee counting ten.
After many trials he vanished from
The ranks of the real contenders.
Now he hangs around the bars and hopes.
Lucky now to be matched in a prelim
With another like himself, a palooka.
One palooka looks at another palooka
And says: he looks like I look.
They tune up the fight fans for the real show,
The bout between two young ones
Of each of whom it is said:
He'll be a champ one of these pretty days.
And every champ that rises from the sawdust ring
Has one fear deeper than any other:
      Look out or you'll be just a palooka.

Green Hair

"The greatest poet of all—Dante," an Italian tells a Frenchman. "Dante—went to hell—and back."

The Frenchman: "Greatest poet of all—Baudelaire—born and raised in hell—and you don't know hell till you read Baudelaire."

Look back and see Baudelaire sitting in a garret, lit up with red hair, writing poems—how he was born and raised in hell before he came to Paris—how lonesome he is—how lonesome everybody is.

Baudelaire one day gets so deep-purple lonesome he goes to a barbershop—comes out with his red hair dyed green— his hair the same as summer grass—summer fern, watercress.

Baudelaire goes to a painter he hates, walks into the studio, takes a chair not saying a word, sits there not saying a word.

The painter stands painting, not saying a word, once in a while slanting his eyes at Baudelaire.

An hour Baudelaire sits there—a long hour—then he stands up: "What the hell is the matter with you? Can't you see I've got green hair?"

The painter goes on like nothing happened, waits a little, turns his head: "What of it? Who cares? A lot of people got green hair. I can see green hair everywhere I go whenever I want to see green hair."

Baudelaire walks out, walks home, walks up the lonesome winding stairs to his garret, takes his pen and writes six new poems—how he was born and raised in hell—how lonesome he is—how lonesome everybody is.

Mulligatawney

The Sioux saying ran, "Love grows like hair on the black
bear's skin; it has a way."
The Arabians spill this, "The first gray hair is a form of
death's challenge."
Read these and remember; bob your hair; or let it go long;
short or long it has a way.
Read an earnest poet, "Life is earnest, let us then be up and
doing."
Or take a tip from Vogner; he did a valkyr music when he
was feeling good once.
Vogner tipped us this, "Climb a tree and hoot like an owl."
Yes, love grows like hair; the first gray hair is a one-word
telegram: bob your hair; be earnest; be a valkyr.
Be a company, a party, a picnic; be alone, a nut, a potato,
an orange blossom, a keg of nails; if you get lost try a
want ad; if night comes try a long sleep.

Mutt Born

McTeague, the mutt,
came from a mutt father
and a mutt mother *fathom (5)*
who met by accident.
We laugh at him.
He gets suspicious,
prowls, kills, slathers.
He hunts the conundrums
of people, jobs, fun, money.
McTeague is our brother,
McTeague, the mutt-born.

[Walt Whitman]

(handwritten annotations: D. Chaney; I celebrate myself / Leaves of Grass myself / I sing myself; Dulce Mornings ill)

Do not discard him because he grew old and preached what
    once he sang. *(the blues ent)*   *"the Goner"*
Do not try to escape him—he is part of you—of all of us. *(pg 141)*
We find him under our bootheels. *(911 attacks)*   *(GGate bridge)*
He sings again in your vision of skyscrapers, workmen,   *Manhattan*
    excavations. *(911)*

Do not deny him because he grew old and preached instead
    of singing.
Jesus of Nazareth might have grown old, and sitting
    helplessly, with dim and rheumy eyes, talked of the
    days when he changed water into wine, days of his
    miracles.
Shelley might not have drowned—but living on, have
    wearied listeners with tales of his revolutionary youth.
Keats might not have died in all the promise of his tragic
    youth, but lived to be a garrulous old man with feverish
    eyes still seeing visions. *(Remote Viewing VB)*
Do not forget him because he grew old and preached what
    once he sang.

Toward The People, Yes

On the undated manuscript of "They Don't Know It Yet," Sandburg wrote: "This was the first draft which grew into The People, Yes." The first draft is a skeleton of what was to become the 180-page poem as it appears in *Complete Poems*. Writing to Alfred Harcourt on November 27, 1935, about the manuscript of *The People, Yes*, Sandburg noted: "I think you will have a large intelligent horselaugh if sometime you compare this final draft of that poem with the first one sent you." Sandburg wrote Malcolm Cowley on January 20, 1935, that the poem, still in progress and then 100 pages long in manuscript, was "the longest piece of verse I have ever done . . . a ballad pamphlet harangue sonata and fugue . . . an almanac, a scroll, a palimpsest, the last will and testament of Mr. John Public, John Doe, Richard Roe, and the autobiography of whoever it was the alfalfa-land governor meant in saying, 'The common people will do anything you say except stay hitched.'"

The poem grew and grew from the one published here to the long version Sandburg finally completed. Through it all, Sandburg believed in the people, just as Steinbeck did in *Grapes of Wrath*. This short version has the power to stand on its own—with appropriate horselaughs, of course.

They Don't Know It Yet

the people is lousy
sure the people is lousy
and this here democracy
is a lot of hooey
more and more baloney
yeah the people is lousy
lissen to the newspapers
morning rags evening rags
the people dont know nothing
never will know nothing
lissen to the big shots
afraid of their shirts
afraid of their utilities
the people dont know nothing
never will know nothing
the people is lousy
yeah that's right say it again
    but lemme tell you this buddy
    let me put one bug in your ear
    let me say this and fade
the people is a big proposition
the people is a mammoth   a behemoth
the people is cyclopean   cyclonic
the people is big with red blood
for one louse   two louses   millions
to live on   fat boys   grifters
the stacked cards   the loaded dice   last only so long
mad when their fixers can't fix it
sore when their toes are stepped on
and the rigged game ain't so hot now

money changers and exploiters no longer
telling the government how and when
they live on the people and like it
they soak in the hot swill of profits
eaten off the blood of the people
swollen profits of extortioners
    and they die and the people live on
    while the big-shot crooks will be dying
    they will croak and go under and be laid away
    and the people will live on
    the lying newspapers will be forgotten
    the cheese editors   the pimp editorial writers
    they will go under the ten-ton truck wheels
    while the people will live on
remembering their friend abe lincoln
remembering their friend frank roosevelt
    yeah the people don't know nothing
    only they know a liar   they know a thief
    they take a long time to learn   to know
    but in time they can tell for sure   bigod
    the respectable liar who lies and lies
    for the sake of big-shot crooks and fixers
    trying to make a comeback
    each an accident   a puff of wind   a short stink
    he can't help what he is no more than a skunk
    and now he and his stinkfingers
    are dropping out of the picture
    and it's curtains   good-night
    and things ain't what they used to be
    and they will be crying-out-loud
    and they will make a high moaning
    and be heard before they go under
the people   buddy   the people will live on

the people is a mammoth   a behemoth
the people is cyclopean   cyclonic
they will stick around a long time yet
they run the works   only they don't know it yet

Works Cited in the Introduction and Commentary

Bruns, Roger A. *The Damndest Radical: The Life and World of Ben Reitman*. Urbana: University of Illinois Press, 1987.

Corwin, Norman. *The World of Carl Sandburg*. New York: Harcourt, Brace and World, 1961.

Detzer, Karl. *Carl Sandburg: A Study in Personality and Background*. New York: Harcourt, Brace and Co., 1941.

Gibbons, Floyd. "'Don' MacGregor Met Death in Mexico Because He 'Stuck' to German Friend." *Chicago Tribune*, April 12, 1916.

Hallwas, John E. "'Fire Flowers': An Uncollected Poem by Carl Sandburg." *Notes on Modern American Literature*, I (Summer 1977), No. 16.

———. Introduction to Sandburg's *Chicago Poems*. Urbana: University of Illinois Press, 1992.

"If Greasers Got MacGregor Labor's Lost a Good Friend," *The Day Book*, April 3, 1916. The unsigned article was probably written by Sandburg.

MacGregor, Don. Letters to Carl Sandburg, March 15, 1914, and April 12, 1914. Sandburg Collection, University of Illinois at Urbana-Champaign Library.

Masters, Edgar Lee. *Across Spoon River: An Autobiography*. New York: Farrar and Rinehart, 1936.

McGovern, George, and Leonard F. Guttridge. *The Great Coalfield War*. Boston: Houghton Mifflin Co., 1972.

Niven, Penelope. *Carl Sandburg: A Biography*. New York: Charles Scribner's Sons, 1991.

Papanikolas, Zeese. *Buried Unsung: Louis Tikas and the*

Ludlow Massacre. Salt Lake City: University of Utah Press, 1982.

Reid, Robert L. *"The Day Book* Poems of Carl Sandburg." *The Old Northwest*, 9 (Fall 1983), 205–218. Reid printed "Sandburg to Loeb" in this article and also in *Battleground: The Autobiography of Margaret A. Haley*, ed. Robert L. Reid. Urbana: University of Illinois Press, 1982.

Sandburg, Carl. *Always the Young Strangers*. New York: Harcourt, Brace and Co., 1953.

———. *Complete Poems of Carl Sandburg*. New York: Harcourt Brace Jovanovich, 1970.

———. *Ever the Winds of Chance*, ed. Margaret Sandburg and George Hendrick. Urbana: University of Illinois Press, 1983.

———. *The Letters of Carl Sandburg*, ed. Herbert Mitgang. New York: Harcourt, Brace and World, 1968.

Sandburg, Margaret, ed. *The Poet and the Dream Girl: The Love Letters of Lilian Steichen and Carl Sandburg*. Urbana: University of Illinois Press, 1987.

Yannella, Philip R. *The Other Carl Sandburg*. Jackson: University Press of Mississippi, 1996.

Index to the Introduction and Commentary

Pages on which the full poems appear are set in italics.

Abraham Lincoln: The Prairie Years, 15
Abraham Lincoln: The War Years, 17, 158
Absolom, 157
"Acknowledgments," 157, *160*
Across Spoon River (Masters), 49
African-Americans, 139–140
"Alice and Phoebe Cary," 87
Always the Young Strangers, 7–8
American Songbag, The, 16
Anti-semitism, 51
Armour, Philip, 157

"Baudelaire and His Green Hat, Mr.," 159
Belshazzar, 157
Berg, Mitchell, 14–15
Billy Sunday and Other Poems (Hendrick), 147
"Billy Sunday," 5, 19, 101–102, *104–106*
Blankenberg, Herman, 26–27
Bolsheviks, 14
"Bonbons," 49, *59*
"Both Ways," 101, *107*
Braithwaite, William Stanley, 6
Bruce, David, 26

"Calamus" (Whitman), 159
Cannibal, The, 10
Carl Sandburg Family Trust, 19
Carranzo government, 26
"Chanting the Square Deific" (Whitman), 157
Charles XII (of Sweden), 158
"Chicago," 3, 9, 18, 79
Chicago, Illinois, 3–4, 6–8, 12–13, 15, 23, 25–26, 47–51, 102, 139, 147–148, 157–158; Gold Coast, 50; Maxwell Street, 48; race riots, 139; West Side, 48
Chicago Board of Education, 50
Chicago Daily News, 16, 47, 128
Chicago Evening World, 13, 23
Chicago Federation of Labor, 50
Chicago Poems, 6, 14, 47, 49
Chicago Teachers' Federation, 50
Chicago Tribune, 23, 26
"Children of Adam" (Whitman), 159

"Christmas Cartoon, 1917," *151*
"Climbers," 157, *162*
Colorado, 8, 23–26, 28
Communism, 14
Complete Poems, 18, 19, 147, 175
Cornhuskers, 14, 28
Corwin, Norman, 70, 79
Cowley, Malcolm, 175
Crane, Stephen, 28–29
"Crayon," 47, *53*

"Daniel Boone," 83, *85*
"[Davvy Tipton]," 83, *89*
Day Book, The, 13, 23–24, 47, 49, 50–51, 101, 147–148
Debs, Eugene, 12
Dell, Floyd, 23
Densmore, Frances, 79
Denver Express, 23, 25
Detzer, Karl, 47, 159
Dial, 4
Dill Pickle Club, 13
"Don MacGregor's Curse," 18, 23–29, *30*
Dreiser, Theodore, 13
"Dynamiter," 5

Edwards, Jonathan, 83
"Elbert Hubbard," *88*
Ever the Winds of Chance, 10
"Everybody in Town Has Been Drillin' and Drillin' for the Big Parade," 147, *152–153*

Fabian movement, 12
"February," *122*
Field, Marshall, 148, 157
"[Finger Pointer]," 101, *108*
Finnish Socialist workers, 15
"Fire Flowers," 37, *43*
"Fires," *121*
"Fleas of Flanders, The," 69, *71–72*
"Fog," 4, 37
Frank, Leo, 51
French Symbolists, 37
Frost, Robert, 17

Galesburg, Illinois, 6–8, 10–11
Gibbons, Floyd P., 23, 26–28
"[Goner, A]," 139, *141*
"Good and Bad Poets," 127, *130*
"Good Woman," 48, *57*
Grapes of Wrath (Steinbeck), 175
"Green Hair," 158, *167–168*

Haley, Margaret, 50
Hallwas, John, 37, 47
Harcourt, Alfred, 5–6, 148, 175
Harvest Poems, 18
Haywood, Big Bill, 13
"[He Sez / I Sez]," 19, 127, *129*
Hearst, William Randolph, 6, 101
Hebrew Institute, 50–51
Helen Haire Levinson Prize, 4
Henderson, Alice Corbin, 3, 5, 27
Henry Holt and Co., 5–6, 101
"[Henry James]," 19, *131–134*
Honey and Salt, 18
Hotel Morrison, 148
Huntington, Collis P., 102

Imagism, 4, 19, 37, 119, 158
In Reckless Ecstasy, 11–12
International Socialist Review,
    13–14, 101
"Iron Jaw," 83, *97*

James, Henry, 127
James, William, 127
Jefferson, Thomas, 6
Jesus (of Nazareth), 6, 128, 157
Johannsen, Anton, 13
"John Arthur Johnson," 139–140, *143*
"John James Audubon," 19, *95*
Johnson, Lyndon, 15
Jones, Jack, 13
Jones, Mother, 25

"Kaltenborn," 102
Kaltenborn, H. V., 102
Kennedy, John F., 15
Kickapoo Indians, 79
Knox College, 11

Lamb, Charles, 158
Labor Defense League, 50
"Last Star, The," *120*
Lenin, Vladimir, 15
Lewis, Sinclair, 13
"Li Po and Lao Tse Come to
    Nebraska," 37, *42*
"[Lilacs of 1917]," *150*
Lincoln, Abraham, 16–17, 175
"Lincoln and His Gloves, Mr." 159
Lindsay, Vachel, 13
Locke, J. H., 26–27
Loeb, Jacob, 50–51
Loeb Rule, 50
Lombard College, 10–11, 13, 16, 127
Lombard Review, The, 10
"Long Shot, A," 50, *62*
"Longfellow and His Boy, Mr." 159
"[Love or Cheap Love]," 139, *142*
"Love Song of J. Alfred Prufrock,
    The" (Eliot), 50

Lowell, Amy, 13, 37–38
"Lower Register, The," 49, *60*
Ludlow Massacre, 25–26, 28
"[Lullaby]," 70, *75*

MacGregor, Don, 13, 23–29
Maggie, A Girl of the Streets
    (Crane), 29
"Magical Confusion," 102
Marx, Karl, 11
Masses, The, 101
Masters, Edgar Lee, 13, 49, 83
Mather, Cotton, 83
"May, 1915," 147, *149*
McGillicuddy, James Aloysius, 48–49
McTeague (Norris), 159
"Memoir of a Proud Boy," 27–28,
    31–33
Mexico, 26
Moir, Harry, 148
Monroe, Harriet, 3–4, 6
"Moon Dance," 37, *39*
Morris, William, 11
"Mulligatawney," 159, *169*
"Mutt Born," 159, *170*

Nebuchadnezzar, 157
New Republic, 37
"New Section," 18, 19
New York City, 4, 8, 15, 147
New York Times, 6
Newspaper Enterprise Association,
    14
Niven, Penelope, 3
Norris, Frank, 159
"November Nocturne," *124*
"Now You Take Her," 49, *58*
Nuroteva, Santeri, 15

"October," *123*
On Account of This Is a Free
    Country," 102, *114–116*
Other Carl Sandburg, The
    (Yannella), 13–14, 101

Palmer, A. Mitchell, 15
Palmer, Mrs. Potter, 47, 102
"Palooka and Champ," 158, *166*
Parsons, Albert R., 102
"[Pass This Baby On]," 79, *80*
Patterson, Joseph Medill, 148
People, Yes, The, 14, 17, 25, 83, 175
Phillips, Jack, 14
"Pie-Wagon Driver, The," 69–70,
    73–74
"Pigeons," 158, *163*
Poems of social protest, 4–6, 14,
    17–18, 37–38, 47–48, 51, 101–103,
    139–140, 148
Poet and the Dream Girl, The, 12

Poetry: A Magazine of Verse, 3–4, 13
Poor Writers' Club, The, 11
"[Portrait of a Lady]," 102, *110–111*
Pound, Ezra, 37
Prostitution, 9, 13, 139–140, 148
Puerto Rico, 9
Pulitzer Prize, 17

"Quotes," 102, *113*

Red Scare, 101
Reid, Robert L., 51, 148
Rockefeller, John D., 23, 26
Rogers, Will, 16
Roosevelt, Franklin Delano, 15
Rootabaga Pigeons, 15
Rootabaga Stories, 15

Sandberg, August, 6–8
Sandberg, Clara, 6–7
Sandburg, Carl: childhood, 6–8, 79; courtship and marriage, 3, 12, 119; education, 8, 9–11; as journalist, 3, 11–17, 23, 28, 47, 101, 127–128; lecture-recitals, 10, 16, 17; Lincoln studies, 15–17, 175; in military, 9; odd jobs, 3, 7–11; as a poet, 17–18, 25–27, 37–38, 47–51, 69–70, 79, 83, 101–103, 127–128, 139–140, 147–148, 157–159, 175; and Pulitzer Prize, 17; Socialist work, 12–14, 23, 25, 47, 49–51, 101, 147–148
Sandburg Collection, 17–19, 79, 102
Sandburg, Janet, 16, 158
Sandburg, Lilian "Paula" Steichen, 3, 12, 119
"Sandburg to Loeb," 50, 51, *65–66*
Sandburg, Margaret, 12, 16, 158
"Selling Spiel [on Maxwell Street]," 48, *56*
Shakespeare, William, 128, 157
Shaw, George Bernard, 12
Shelley, Percy Bysshe, 26, 28–29
Sjodin, John, 7–8, 11
Slabs of the Sunburnt West, 14
Smoke and Steel, 14
Social Democratic party, 12
Socialism, 5, 7–8, 11–15, 23, 25–26, 101, 147
Socrates, 83
"Socrates," 19, *90–91*
Song of Myself (Whitman), 49, 159
Spanish-American War, 9–10
"Speed Bug," 48, *55*
Spoon River Anthology (Masters), 83
Stalin, Joseph, 14
Steichen, Edward, 3, 12
Steinbeck, John, 175

"Stephen Crane," *92*
"Stephen Pearl Andrews," *96*
Stories for children, 15–16
"Studio Sunday Afternoon," 49–50, 61
"Successful Films," 128, *135*
"Sunday," 37, *40*
Sunday, Billy, 5–6, 83, 101–102, 148
Sweden, 6–7, 14–16

"Talk with God, A," 102, *112*
Terre Haute, 83
"Terry Hut," 19, 83, *84*
Thaw, Harry, 157
"Theodosia Burr," *86*
"They Don't Know It Yet," 175, *176–178*
Tietjens, Eunice, 3–4
Tikas, Louis, 25
"To a Contemporary Bunkshooter," 5–6, 101
"[Tom Edison]," *94*
Tomorrow Magazine, 12
Trelawny, Edward John, 28
Truman, Harry, 15
Twain, Mark, 16
"Two Girls and a Father," 158, *165*
"Two Shapes in Gray," 158, *164*
"[Two-Dollars-a-Day Wop]," 47, *52*

Universalist church, 10
University of Illinois at Urbana-Champaign, 17, 19, 79

Villa, Pancho, 26, 28

Wafflehorn, 102
"Wafflehorn," 102–103
Wagner, Richard, 159
"[Walt Whitman]," 19, *171*
"When Lilacs Last at the Dooryard Bloom'd" (Whitman), 159
White, Stanford, 157
Whitman, Walt, 4, 9, 11–12, 49, 157, 159
"Who Was Hannah Adams?" *93*
"[Wilderness Man]," 47–48, *54*
Wilson, Woodrow, 14, 147
"Wings," 37, *41*
Wisconsin, 12–13, 23
"Woman on the Billboards, The," 148, *154*
World of Carl Sandburg, The (Corwin), 70, 79
World War I, 13–14, 18, 26, 69, 101, 147–148
"[Wreck a Bank]," 102, *109*
Wright, Philip Green, 10–12

Yannella, Philip R., 13–14, 101
"Young Woman," 50, *63–64*

Sandburg's
on Kansas time

A NOTE ON THE EDITORS

George Hendrick is professor of English at the University of Illinois at Urbana-Champaign; Willene Hendrick is his wife and an independent scholar. Over many years the Hendricks have been closely associated with the Sandburg estate and have worked with the large Sandburg Collection at the University of Illinois. Together they have edited *Selected Poems of Carl Sandburg, Billy Sunday and Other Poems,* and *The Savour of Salt,* and have written *Katherine Anne Porter.* George Hendrick has also edited Sandburg's *More Rootabagas* and *To Reach Eternity: The Letters of James Jones.*